Praise for *Smarter Spending*

"Creating strong links in the supply chain is one of the hidden keys of any successful and resilient business. Procurement is not just about saving costs. In Smarter Spending, Neil Apter and Pedro Amendoeira, lead you to a wider view of how firms build their competitive advantage."

Dr Manuel Caldeira Cabral, PhD (Nottingham), Professor of Economics, University of Minho (former Portuguese Economic Minister)

"Smarter Spending is a timely and highly practical guide for leaders who want to improve profitability without undermining long-term value. Drawing on deep, real-world experience, Neil Apter and Pedro Amendoeira move the conversation beyond blunt cost cutting and into thoughtful, principles led decision-making that strengthens organisations rather than hollowing them out. The book combines strategic clarity with actionable insight, challenging assumptions while remaining firmly grounded in commercial reality. For executives serious about resilience, sustainability, and smarter use of capital, this is an essential read."

Carla Rebelo, Global Head of Adecco Permanent Recruitment, SVP

"Smarter Spending is a game-changer for understanding how organizations can make better spending decisions and transform their approach to procurement to build stronger, more value-driven companies – brought to life through real-world stories."

Joana Silva, PhD, Deputy Chief Economist at the World Bank and Associate Professor at Catolica Lisbon School of Economics and Management

"Congratulations to the authors Pedro and Neil for this comprehensive and didactic book. In my view, there is a systemic perspective in which everything is interconnected. We are able to gain a broader understanding and increase our ability to see that businesses, teams, and clients form an indivisible whole. It is truly a book that leads us to notice extremely important details that we are not aware of in our daily lives."

Antonio Raab, Entrepreneur and Senior Advisor, former Board Member of the Hilti Foundation, Hilti's General Manager in Portugal and Brasil

AF631503

"An engaging and insightful read, full of real-world stories that make procurement come alive. Whether you're new to the field or a seasoned sourcing professional, this book offers both inspiration and a powerful reminder of the core principles that drive success."

David Rickard, Former Senior Global Procurement Director, Microsoft

"What struck me about Smarter Spending is how deeply human and practical it is. Neil and Pedro take a subject many leaders shy away from and turn it into clear, common-sense mindsets that apply as much to running a household or a small business as they do to large organisations. The book treats spending as a human challenge, not a numeric one – a matter of behaviour, clarity, and making smarter choices. And on that level, every leader and decision-maker will recognise themselves in these pages."

Pellegrino Riccardi, Award-winning Tedx & Global Keynote Speaker

"I love it. This book is chock-full of excellent advice, illustrated with wonderful examples that bring the authors' points to life. At its core are ten principles. And these are principles for the ages. Who could doubt that adhering to them will not just save your organisation money but build a more resilient business."

Mike Clayton, Author and Founder, Online PM Courses

"Smarter Spending challenges leaders to see costs and overheads not as limitations, but as signals of strategy and purpose. Its ten principles offer a clear, practical way to align every pound with intent. As a purposeful B Corp, this mindset is essential: how we spend must reflect what we stand for. This book provides a great framework for turning operational spend into genuine strategic advantage."

James Sandford, Managing Director, Propellernet, a B Corp

"Smarter Spending is a refreshingly practical book for business leaders. It gives CEOs, boards, and procurement teams tools they can use immediately to make better decisions – while quietly reminding us that how organisations spend reveals what they truly value, and who they really are."

Stuart Marginson, Managing Director & Founder, Highgate

Smarter Spending

Pearson

At Pearson, we have a simple mission: to help people make more of their lives through learning.

We combine innovative learning technology with trusted content and educational expertise to provide engaging and effective learning experiences that serve people wherever and whenever they are learning.

From classroom to boardroom, our curriculum materials, digital learning tools and testing programmes help to educate millions of people worldwide – more than any other private enterprise.

Every day our work helps learning flourish, and wherever learning flourishes, so do people.

To learn more, please visit us at **www.pearson.com**

Smarter Spending

Improve profit through cost optimisation

Pedro Amendoeira and Neil Apter

Pearson

Harlow, England • London • New York • Boston • San Francisco • Toronto • Sydney
Dubai • Singapore • Hong Kong • Tokyo • Seoul • Taipei • New Delhi
Cape Town • São Paulo • Mexico City • Madrid • Amsterdam • Munich • Paris • Milan

PEARSON EDUCATION LIMITED
KAO Two
KAO Park
Harlow CM17 9NA
United Kingdom
Tel: +44 (0)1279 623623
Web: www.pearson.com

First edition published 2026 (print and electronic)

© Pearson Education Limited 2026 (print and electronic)

The rights of Neil Apter and Pedro Amendoeira to be identified as authors of this work have been asserted by them in accordance with the Copyright, Designs and Patents Act 1988.

The print publication is protected by copyright. Prior to any prohibited reproduction, storage in a retrieval system, distribution or transmission in any form or by any means, electronic, mechanical, recording or otherwise, permission should be obtained from the publisher or, where applicable, a licence permitting restricted copying in the United Kingdom should be obtained from the Copyright Licensing Agency Ltd, Barnard's Inn, 86 Fetter Lane, London EC4A1EN.

The ePublication is protected by copyright and must not be copied, reproduced, transferred, distributed, leased, licensed or publicly performed or used in any way except as specifically permitted in writing by the publishers, as allowed under the terms and conditions under which it was purchased, or as strictly permitted by applicable copyright law. Any unauthorised distribution or use of this text may be a direct infringement of the authors' and the publisher's rights and those responsible may be liable in law accordingly.

All trademarks used herein are the property of their respective owners. The use of any trademark in this text does not vest in the author or publisher any trademark ownership rights in such trademarks, nor does the use of such trademarks imply any affiliation with or endorsement of this book by such owners.

Pearson Education is not responsible for the content of third-party internet sites.

ISBN: 978-1-292-76324-8 (print)
978-1-292-49554-5 (ePub)

British Library Cataloguing-in-Publication Data
A catalogue record for the print edition is available from the British Library

Library of Congress Cataloging-in-Publication Data
A catalog record for the print edition is available from the Library of Congress

10 9 8 7 6 5 4 3 2 1
30 29 28 27 26

Cover design by Kelly Miller

Print edition typeset in 10/14 pt Charter ITC Pro regular by Straive
Printed by Bell and Bain Ltd, Glasgow

NOTE THAT ANY PAGE CROSS REFERENCES REFER TO THE PRINT EDITION

Contents

Author's acknowledgments

Pedro

To the remarkable women in my family who make my life richer and fuller: Mónica, Sílvia, Maria Emília and Susana.

To my team Carla, Sofia and Herbert, for creating the space that made this work possible.

To Esther Gongora, who introduced me to ERA Group and encouraged me to take a path that proved formative.

To Carlos Nunes, whose mentorship in the early years shaped much of what followed.

To our ERA Group colleagues, whose commitment to creating value for clients continues to inspire. In particular, Paulo Barros, Sara Freitas, João Porto, Vasco Freitas, Inês Lessa, Luís Dionísio, João Pontes, João Costa, Patricia Moreira, Pedro Ramalho, Manuel Velazquez, Juan Garza, Lucia Aguirre, Octavio Barceló, Chemari Linares and David Bertomeu.

My sincere thanks also to Nuno Magalhães for his thoughtful and steady support.

And to my friends, for your enduring encouragement and loyalty.

Neil

Above all, to my family. Most of all to my wife Hayley, for being everything, and to the fab four: Danielle, Shannon, Caitlin and Eden – all of you are my privilege. Thank you for your patience, understanding and unwavering encouragement throughout this process.

To my parents, for instilling the curiosity and resilience that underpin this work. To my brothers, in-laws and nieces and nephews on both sides, your presence and support are deeply valued.

I am grateful particularly to Chris, who helped me finally find my place, and to Rob and colleagues in Southampton, as well as to those across Kent, the UK and Europe, whose perspectives have influenced my thinking over many years.

I am particularly thankful to Jason for the initial impetus, and to Dave, Stu, Jimmy, Mike and Pellegrino for their early review and constructive challenge, which materially strengthened this manuscript.

My thanks also to Peter and Rachel, and to Marc and Anthony, for their legal guidance and considered advice.

Neil and Pedro

Together, we extend our thanks to Fred Marfleet and to ERA teams past and present, with whom we have shared the privilege of working alongside exceptional colleagues. We would especially like to thank our early readers - Henk, Manuel, Andrea, Neil, James, Chris, Tony, JD, Peter & Martti.

We are grateful to Eloise Cook, Lou Atwood, Yashmeena Bisht, Amer Parikh and the wider team at Pearson for their professionalism, guidance and belief in this project.

Finally, to the organisations and clients who entrusted us with access to their companies and decision-making environments, your challenges gave this book its purpose.

To anyone we may have unintentionally omitted, please accept our sincere thanks nonetheless; any omission is one of memory, not appreciation.

How to use this book

As well as our principles-based framework, we've developed practical tools that help you to embed the lessons from the book. None of them are complicated, and you will be familiar with the design underneath them all. These simple frameworks are designed to apply in any organisation, large or small, in any sector and are our way of codifying the knowledge and experience we've gained.

The tools we've developed alongside this book capture, structure and share our accumulated insight, so that it can be applied more consistently and effectively by you.

We hope that by introducing them to you, they can become a shared language for better decision-making. Think of them as a starting point: a set of flexible aids that enable you to start conversations, diagnose opportunities and reflect on how spending works in your world.

Here's what you will find in the Appendix: Activating smarter spending at the end of this book.

- *the Smarter Spending Diagnostic & Radar tool:* a self-assessment tool designed to gauge where you stand against our ten principles;
- *the Smarter Spending Matrix:* a 2×2 grid to chart where spend is adding value – and where it's draining it;
- *the Principles Mapping Canvas:* a one-page tool to map how each principle shows up (or doesn't) in your project, team or organisation;
- *the Enough / Optimal threshold tool:* a short exercise to look at what constitutes sufficiency in your business.

You can use these tools on your own, with your team or as part of a workshop. For a small business, you can use them for an hour and document it all on a whiteboard. For larger organisations, they can be an anchor for deeper reviews and strategy sessions. And, of course, you can contact us to help.

We're also happy to acknowledge our debt to Peter Kraljic's 1983 matrix published in the *Harvard Business Review*. It has provided an operational framework for procurement for decades. It asks: 'How important is this item, and how risky is its supply?'. Forty years on, we're asking a different question: 'What purpose does this spend serve, and what value does it destroy or create?'. It's less of a grid and more of a compass to help you navigate systemic change, helping you decide not just what you buy, but who you become by doing so.

You do not have to use these tools – the book stands on its own as stories, examples, reflections and the odd cautionary tale. But if you do want to take the next step, look also at the Appendix and use these tools to test your biases, check your thinking and discuss with your colleagues how well you are putting the principles into practice.

You can enjoy the book, but the real value of smarter spending comes not from reading about it, but by applying it in your own businesses, to see where clarity, control and smarter spending decisions can take you.

Finally, we would like to take a moment to thank all the wonderful colleagues, past and present, who we have worked with, talked to and learned from over the years, whose knowledge, experience and wisdom have inspired us to write this book.

Pedro Amendoeira and Neil Apter

chapter 1

Introduction

1.1 Why you need this book

In most businesses, Sales and Marketing take centre stage. The boss often visits their main clients, plans events to keep them happy and worries about how to best communicate the company's image and brand. It's the attractive part of the business, the one that gets celebrated and wins awards. Production, HR and Finance also get the necessary attention. Often Procurement comes at the bottom of the list.

Suppliers are rarely visited, supplier events are by comparison few and far between and too little attention tends to be paid to how to communicate effectively with suppliers, especially in overhead or overlooked areas. Despite these obvious red flags, many companies assume they are doing fine with cost and supplier management, and that the prices they get are just the costs of doing business.

In *Gulliver's Travels* the eponymous hero finds himself shipwrecked on Lilliput, an island where the inhabitants are only six inches tall. The Lilliputians see all of Gulliver's imperfections magnified. If you look thoroughly and closely enough at something you are bound to find faults and ways to improve. If you don't look particularly closely, it's easier to just trust that things are running fine.

The truth is that room for improvement exists in every company, in every area of the business. But because Procurement often comes last, the best opportunities to create value all too often remain unexplored. It's a costly mistake. Procurement has the power to add considerable value to organisations that empower it. Years ago, most functions were focused on driving down cost. Now, they focus on generating value, by using their valuable insight and expertise to influence organisational policy and procedure too.

That so many small and medium-sized enterprises (SMEs) in particular lack this focus is especially surprising, because every pound, euro or dollar saved goes straight to the bottom line. By contrast, sell another pound and it likely will cost you 90 pence, depending on your margin. To put it another way, another dollar of growth yields just 10 cents of profit, but every dollar you save through smarter spending drops straight to the bottom line. Not only are great opportunities hidden in Procurement, their impact on results is also greater *and* more immediate. No sales pipeline required: just real impact on the bottom line – fast.

Modern-day procurement knowledge can add substantial value to any organisation if it is respected, resourced correctly and allowed serious engagement early. There are a ton of things organisations can do by becoming better at dealing with suppliers and none of them involve beating them up for price. Procurement is not about negotiation per se, although sometimes negotiation skills can come in handy.

In our combined experience of over 30 years, we have contributed to hundreds of companies of all dimensions improving their profits through cost optimisation. In this book we use the knowledge and practice we and our peers have accumulated to explore all the ways in which any company can increase its results through smart purchasing, regardless of its dimension. Whether you turnover €1 million, €10 million, €100 million or €1 billion, these are valuable, practical insights that can help you become more efficient, more resilient, more profitable and more sustainable.

This book is aimed at managing directors, general managers, CEOs, CFOs, COOs and financial controllers, as well as procurement professionals in private, public and third sector organisations. It's also aimed at anyone else that can influence a company's strategies and actions, including third-party advisors. We will share the strategies and methods to help you with your task of improving your company and its results through more effective procurement.

As everything continues to get more expensive, actively managing rising costs can make a tangible difference to your profit margin. It could make the difference between getting through the next crisis and not. As you will discover, this book is underpinned by a set of beliefs. We believe that by embracing them, you can change your mindset, change your organisation's approach to spending and change your future for the better.

We also believe that work, learning and fun should go together, so we will use stories and analogies to get our message out and hope you will enjoy reading this book. Thinking more intentionally about spending is packed with opportunities and can deliver worthwhile results.

We're not saying that nobody has any focus on costs – of course they do. The question is: is your organisation focused enough? Is the balance between chasing perpetual growth and higher sales and actively managing spend right? In our experience, it tends to be a little off.

As we realised during the process of writing and structuring this book, behind every smarter spending decision is a way of thinking. A mindset that emerged over time, from the hundreds of projects, thousands of conversations and millions of pounds / dollars / euros of spending reviewed. Certain patterns kept on showing up. We saw them when things went right – and when they went wrong. Eventually we gave them names.

These are *the ten principles of smarter spending* – ways of thinking that emphasise the importance of focus on procurement; ideas that help leaders, teams and organisations spend with clarity and intention.

They are not a fixed methodology or a prescriptive checklist. We also hope you'll realise, as we have, that this lens enables you to make better decisions in all sorts of interesting ways.

You won't see them in every chapter, but references to their relevance and application are scattered throughout the book. Once you can recall them, you – like us – will start to spot them everywhere. They are designed to help you ask better questions; challenge established assumptions; and ensure spend is connected to the mission.

Used individually or in combination, these principles support a mindset shift, from antipathy to engagement, and from reactive cost-cutting to purpose-driven investment: from 'what can we trim?' to 'what are we trying to achieve?'.

These techniques help clients to save money while building more resilient businesses. Now, we hope they can do the same for you. We also hope you will realise, as we have, that you can use these principles as a lens through which you can also make better decisions with your own spending and start to think about how this thinking could benefit society.

Throughout the book, we'll provide reminders of the links to these principles, a range of relevant questions you can ask yourself and provide ideas for exercises you can use to run with your own teams. By the end, you will be able to examine what your spending really looks like and understand how much smarter it could be.

1.2 Let go of assumptions

This chapter applies the 2,500-year-old parable of the jungle raft: the thing that saved you can become the thing that holds you back. It is a call to question what you are carrying forward by default.

A Buddhist parable tells of a man who is alone and lost in the jungle. He is without food, water and shelter. He is frightened, aware of the dangers that surround him.

The man reaches a river, too wide to swim. He realises that the once foreboding jungle can provide the resources that he needs to reach safety on the other side. Exhausted, he begins to pull together the makings of a raft. He makes it across the river, where he finds food and safety.

Having expected to die, the man was extremely grateful to the raft that had saved him. The dilemma pondered by the Buddha was whether the man should take the raft with him on his onward journey or discard it at the riverbank.

Important though it was, you can imagine the inconvenience and disruption that taking this raft everywhere would cause him. The Buddha's teaching was that, although the raft had been important, it should not be held onto once it had served its purpose.

It was a metaphor for his followers to encourage them to allow themselves to let go of their beliefs and continually open themselves to letting go of their old thoughts to reach new ways of understanding. He had to let go of the raft. Do not let that which once worked for you become a burden that you keep carrying around with you.

We start here because this is something that we see happening in businesses all the time.

The business raft: How solutions become baggage

What works at the personal level, can often become enterprise-wide behaviour. Imagine the scenario – we could really be talking here about anything inside an organisation. A problem arises, a solution is found: a new part, a new piece of machinery, a new member of staff, a new team, a new project, a new waste solution, a new delivery partner, a new raw materials supplier.

Sometimes, not always, but often enough for it to be a serious problem, the solutions that we find – especially when reacting to problems – become the 'rafts' that the organisation begins to carry into all sort of inappropriate situations. When we talk to clients about why this happens, the refrain is familiar: *'It is just how we do things'*.

But the world changes constantly. Perhaps no more so than lately. To be lean, you need to react. When the environment changes around you, you must change with it. After all, what good is a raft to cross a desert? Or a street? The right solution is needed at every turn, for each job. The market means there are always optimal solutions available, so how often should you test it, and in which areas? What is the right balance between supplier loyalty and reviewing the market?

Regardless of how successful you or your company are at this point, you are sure to carry some beliefs, methods, processes or suppliers that were once useful, but that are now more likely to be holding you back, rather than helping you to progress.

Ask yourself: 'What rafts are we carrying?'.

It can be an important reminder and highlights the fact that we are often unconsciously carrying that extra weight. During his epic speech in the first episode of Aaron Sorkin's '*The Newsroom*' on HBO, Jeff Bridges' Will McAvoy, states: 'The first step in solving any problem is recognising there is one.' Socrates insisted that 'the only true wisdom is in knowing you know nothing.'

Most consultants are invited into companies to help them solve a specific problem. However, many of the organisations that could benefit from using the kind of strategic cost management services we provide often do not believe that they need to, until we come along.

The best way of uncovering these things within organisations is to have constant and careful analysis of your current situation. The most efficient and effective organisations are constantly vigilant, open-minded and always questioning the status quo.

The more these rafts become 'part of the cost of doing business', the more the carrier cannot see what is on their backs. We can all be full of ideas about how to improve someone else's work rather than reflecting on ourselves. It is much easier to see the rafts on other people's backs.

The parable of the raft also provides another insight: it wasn't even the best way to cross the river. It was simply what the man could build at the time with what he had. A bridge or a boat would have made him safe quicker.

He clung to the raft in part because he'd built it with his own hands. The behavioural economist Dan Ariely calls this limitation the 'Ikea effect'– people placing a higher value on the things they produce themselves, even when there are better options available.

That same emotional attachment can cloud business judgement. Letting go of something that is 'yours', whether that's a policy, a system or a supplier, can feel like letting go of a piece of yourself.

Pride makes us defend what we've built. But defending it blindly can weigh us down. 'It's just how we've always done things' is often code for 'we're attached to what we know', but habits, however familiar, should not be sacred cows, and improvement usually demands that we look beyond what is comfortable.

To get the most out of reading this book, you will need to put your ego and your relationships to one side and focus on what is objectively true. We're not here to criticise what you've done, only to help you to see what could be better.

You'll learn how to question your tools, challenge your defaults and sharpen your decisions, particularly around suppliers and cost. You'll see that small, painless changes can eliminate big mistakes, unlock value and free your business to move forward unencumbered, with clarity of purpose.

Throughout the chapters ahead, we'll refer to this set of core principles – a kind of operating philosophy – practical ideas shaped by experience. You won't need to memorise them. But you'll start to see how a few powerful ideas, such as '*Challenge Assumptions*', can shape radically better decisions. This book is also designed to get you thinking about questions like 'what rafts are we carrying – and why?'. What are your inherited ways of spending or structuring processes and costs that once (probably) served a purpose but now require attention?

Activity

Use our 'Enough/Optimal' tool in the Appendix to review your own legacy spends. To review the cost rafts you are carrying, first decide how to perform the exercise. Depending on the complexity and nature of your business, you might want to run this based on direct and indirect spend, or by department. Decide who needs to be involved in terms of supplying the data you need, and whether to invite them to the meeting.

1.3 What the space race can teach us about cost

Organisations are drawn to comforting myths about simplicity and clever shortcuts. Behind every story of innovation lies discipline, curiosity, and rigorous problem-solving.

During the Cold War, the US and USSR competed on every front. Nowhere was this more visible than in the space race. In 1961, the Soviets put the first man in space and in 1969, with people gathered around TV sets, the US put the first man on the moon.

To do so, they both had to solve thousands of engineering problems. One of them was seemingly simple. How would their cosmonauts and astronauts record their activity? Pens work by the action of gravity over the ink, forcing it down onto the surface. Write upside down for too long and the ink runs dry. In space, without gravity, a pen is useless.

To try and solve the conundrum, NASA spent millions trying to develop a pen that was able to write in space. To solve the same problem, the Soviets just used pencils.

Or so the story goes.

You may have heard it at a seminar or read it in a newspaper or a book. The story is held up as a symbol of how simple solutions are often the best, and that sometimes you can find them right in front of you.

As is often the case with these apocryphal tales, it did not quite happen the way it has been told. Pencils (even mechanical pencils) are a lousy way to write in space. Lead can break and splinter and sharpening a pencil leaves all sort of fine debris. You do not want these things floating around in zero gravity on a spaceship, liable to get into the wrong nooks and crannies, with the potential to interfere with precision equipment.

Writing with pencil lead can easily become blurred, which is far from ideal when you are taking notes on precision measurements. On top of that, graphite is flammable, a characteristic probably best avoided in materials aboard spaceships.

Although it is true that NASA has spent time trying to develop a pen able to write in space *and failed*, in the meantime they were of course using pencils themselves as well as the Soviets, who had simply given up earlier on that path of development.

In 1965 a US inventor and engineer called Paul C. Fisher finally solved the problem. He patented a pen that uses nitrogen to pressurise the ink, pushing it towards a tungsten tip. Besides being able to write without gravity, it can also write upside down, underwater, over grease around even in widely varying extreme temperatures.

It even lasts three times longer than most pens and has an estimated shelf life of 100 years. Back then, NASA tested the pen, saw its potential and in 1967 they bought 400 pens. Ever since then, it has been used on all US space missions, including the moon landings. Anyone can still buy them from the Fisher Space Pen company website today.

Paul Fisher created the pen by his own volition, with his own means, without grants or subsidies of any kind. The problem was solved by a man with entrepreneurial spirit, willing to keep searching until he found a valid solution. Neither Soviet central planning, nor the might of American sub-contracting were able to get there.

We believe that both the real story and the urban myth we started this chapter with provide a few valuable insights.

The story of Paul C. Fisher and his Space Pen is less known than the story about the pencil because people are suckers for a nice story. We love easy, memorable caricatures and a stereotypical cast. But while we caricature the overspending US bureaucrats and the thrifty Soviets, we should be aware that most of us are prone to this type of bias.

Stories are fundamentally human. They have been told for tens of thousands of years, and they are how we communicate and how we see ourselves. They are an amazing way to spread a message both in business and in life.

But if we are making decisions based on stories, they should be based on *true* stories: on facts. Over the years, time and again, we have seen that the stories that are told within companies and believed for years, often have *no* basis in fact. One colleague went to work at a ceramics factory, where it was known by all that the ovens could not be turned off at the weekends, or disaster would strike.

Whatever had happened in the past, when our colleague *challenged* this *assumption* and turned them off at weekends, nothing untoward happened. The worry was unnecessary. The story was untrue. No more wasted cash on energy at the weekend. Savings generated by testing a long-held assumption. The stories repeated most often, the basis on which decisions are made, are not always true. Testing assumptions can get tiresome, but there is no doubt that it produces great results.

Stories like this illustrate why organisations often turn to outside help for a different perspective. Getting to the facts demands an independence that is hard to have if you live inside the daily reality. A fresh pair of eyes can help. Investing in innovation inside the business can strengthen from within, but sometimes you need a Paul C. Fisher.

Consultants engage with different organisations and how they do things. We regularly find fantastic examples of best practice, innovative thinking and ingenious solutions that can be applied elsewhere.

We often also find organisations living with the equivalent of that pencil in space, or the 24/7 oven. It kind of works, but it causes other problems. After a while, we all tend to accept these problems as facts of life and not even think about them. In most cases, these problems are solvable, sometimes in surprisingly simple ways.

These types of problems are sometimes best resolved by looking somewhere other than the obvious places. What is normally most effective is introducing collaborators, perhaps from other departments and looking at the problem from a different angle.

The space pen reminds us that stories become habits and habits become expensive. Sometimes, what we need is not more of the same, but a completely different question – asked by someone who isn't usually in the room. Whether it's our suppliers, friends, colleagues in a different department, or an outside partner, the solution to your problem probably already exists. Only invent the wheel if you need to – as we will see later.

Throughout this book, we will show you more stories like this. They will help you to uncover your own pencils in space: things that do a job but could be better. When you start questioning what you've previously accepted as fact, you unlock the potential to do more with fewer resources. You may even create your own space pen and fine-tune your company or department into a vessel that can reach for the stars.

1.4 Looking for problems with the wrong tools

The most damaging costs are often hidden, not visible on the balance sheet or obvious to leadership. Organisations need to develop the tools to diagnose invisible inefficiencies before they escalate.

On 2 July 1881, four months after his inauguration, while preparing to board a train in Washington DC, President James Garfield was shot twice, one bullet grazing his arm and another penetrating his back and lodging somewhere in the abdomen.

His assassin was Charles J. Guiteau. After helping with Garfield's campaign, he was expecting to be rewarded with a job in the administration. When no such offer was forthcoming, he decided to react in the most extreme way. He was caught immediately and executed a year later.

The president took some time to die. After being shot, he was taken upstairs in the railway station, apparently conscious, but in shock. He was then carried back to the White House and told he was unlikely to last the night. Garfield made it through the night, and in fact much longer.

The US population waited for updates on his condition throughout the summer. The best minds in the country were brought in to help try to save the president. These included the best doctors and even naval engineers, who created an air-cooling device, the first air conditioning unit, to cool the feverish president's room in the summer heat.

The problem was that the bullet, which was lodged somewhere within his body, could not be found. To try to establish the location of the bullet, Alexander Graham Bell – the lauded inventor and one of the greatest geniuses of the time – was brought in. During the process of inventing the telephone, he had developed a metal-detector, which he believed would be instrumental in locating the bullet.

When he applied the apparatus on the president's body it pinged immediately. Lucky first guess? Just to be sure, Bell moved it around and it kept detecting metal, going off all over the president's body. Only months later did the scientist realise what had happened: the machine detected every steel spring in the mattress. In the meantime, Garfield died. Not from the bullet wound itself, but from an infection because his body had been moved around too much as physicians – and a telephony pioneer – looked for the bullet.

In this case, the failure to have the right tool to solve the problem and no precedent to follow had tragic consequences. Over the years of working in our capacity with companies, we have seen many otherwise brilliant people using metal detectors to look for a bullet on a box spring mattress.

Nobody can be good at everything. Nobody can think of every eventuality, always. People make mistakes. People do things because it seems like a good idea, because they're not thinking about it deeply, or because it has always been done that way.

Although some management techniques and principles have become universal, many organisations still use bespoke processes and 'homemade' solutions, simply because they feel like they own them. Particularly during the good times, when the company's results are good, we tend not to question the processes.

But continuously challenging these surface-level assumptions is fundamental to achieving success and, even more difficult, to maintaining it. Peter Drucker, one of the great management gurus, once said his job was to be paid to ask stupid questions. He was right, it sometimes takes an outsider to ask the questions we should be asking ourselves; ask any therapist.

For whatever reason, people tend to find it extremely difficult, both individually and collectively, to query existing ways of thinking. The questions for each of you and your organisations will be different, but they should be asked, because you never know when you might need to find your own bullet. As well as Garfield, Lincoln and Kennedy, there were assassination attempts on Andrew

Jackson, Theodore Roosevelt and Ronald Reagan. We will not include the attempt in 2024 on Trump, who was campaigning at the time.

Though the guns of Jacksons' would-be assassin failed, Roosevelt and Reagan *were* both shot and injured. So although US Bureau of Labour Statistics might tell you that logging is the most hazardous occupation in the US, it seems that if you become president, you have roughly a one in eight chance of taking a bullet on the job and then more than a 50% chance the bullet will kill you.

In turbulent times, companies don't just need to dodge bullets; they need to design systems that can absorb shocks and adapt quickly to survive the unexpected. That means asking better questions. It means having access to the right data and using the right tools to make the correct diagnosis. It means being able to challenge the way things have always been done, *especially* when they appear to be working fine.

Garfield died because brilliant people used the wrong tools on the wrong problem. If you don't challenge what you think you know, it doesn't matter how well-intentioned, brilliant or lucky you are.

chapter 2

The ten principles of smarter spending

These are the definitions of the ten principles. How you choose to use them is up to you. You may decide to use them all, or only some of them. You may decide to reframe them to fit the work you do, or the ways in which you work.

However you approach the ten principles, adapt them and apply them, remember that they have come from an observance of practice in businesses and organisations like yours. They are designed to make you more considered and intentional in your approach to how cost and therefore spending work within your company.

2.1 Spend with purpose

If you don't know why you're spending, you won't know when to stop – just ask any gambler. In theory, every pound spent by a business should connect back to strategy. In practice, most organisations cannot link their day-to-day spend to their overarching objectives. But they should ensure they are only spending money if that spend is contributing to their overall goals. Anything else is just waste.

From punitive legacy supply contracts to outdated budget allocations, misaligned spending is endemic. It is rarely malicious or even due to incompetence; it's just… unconscious.

We've observed this time after time. Teams are often delivering against their budgets, so it looks like there is nothing wrong. But within these functional silos, there is no shared sense of why a given spend matters. One team continues to invest heavily in training for a system marked for phase-out. Another spends extortionate sums with an agency to rebrand, while ignoring the fact that their brand is people's perception of their customer experience, not the logo and their fulfilment department was making them haemorrhage customers. In both cases, the spending wasn't driving outcomes, it was just happening without communication.

> In 1979 in the UK, British Rail was looking for a new agency partner to handle business. Up against the might of the industry, a smaller agency called ABM was invited to pitch. Scheduled for a 10 a.m. meeting on the day, the train executives show up five minutes early and report to reception. The receptionist gestured towards a seated waiting area while talking on the phone.
>
> The seating area was littered with dirty coffee cups, old magazines and ashtrays overflowing with cigarette butts (this was the 70s!). Ten o'clock came and went, so the lead exec approached reception again and asked how long they would be made to wait and was again largely ignored. After a huddle in reception, appalled at their treatment, they gathered their coats and bags to leave.
>
> At which point, the boardroom doors burst open, and Peter Marsh (the 'M' in ABM) came out. Looking them right in the eye he said 'Gentlemen, you now understand how the British public feel about British Rail, now let's show you how we're going to put it right.'

Marsh demonstrates that you must know the problem you are trying to fix, or there's no point spending anything. To *Spend with Purpose* is to ensure every cost has a clear link to a defined goal. It means mapping spend categories to strategic priorities: growth, efficiency, customer experience, resilience. It means rejecting the idea that being under budget is a virtue. You must know – are you under budget on the things that matter, or on things that don't? This principle forces the uncomfortable but vital conversation: *Is this the best use of capital, right now?*

Spend with Purpose doesn't mean austerity. It may justify spending more if it's deliberate: when you're clear on what you're trying to achieve, cost control becomes a lever, not a leash.

2.2 See the whole system

Silos are expensive. Blind spots, more so. Business doesn't happen in straight lines – it happens in systems. Yet many cost decisions are made in isolation. A procurement team celebrates shaving 8% off software support costs. A customer service team suddenly struggles with faulty inputs. Somewhere along the chain, nobody connected the dots.

This principle emerged because we watched small wins drive big losses. A university client renegotiated catering costs, only to suffer complaints that impacted enrolment events. A manufacturer found a cheaper component supplier, but delivery inconsistencies disrupted production. No one intended harm. But no one had system visibility either.

> Optimising spending in isolation, or in specific areas, without considering the wider whole is like pulling a thread from an old sweater. It can make the whole thing fall apart. Cheaper secondary packaging may seem like a way to cut costs, but may also increase breakages, returns and customer complaints. What looks like a saving has in fact cost you.
>
> Whack-a-mole procurement does no good. Beating things down and into shape is not fixing the system, it's asking for other problems to pop up elsewhere.

See the Whole System means tracing costs across departments, stakeholders and time. It means knowing what happens *after* a decision has been made. Which team bears the knock-on costs, who puts up with the unintended delays caused by a decision and, ultimately, whose job is it to clean it up?

This mindset moves procurement from reactive to proactive, from isolated to strategic. It lets you forecast value across the lifecycle, not just at the point of purchase. It also improves collaboration. When teams share an understanding of how costs ripple, they coordinate better, faster. The businesses that thrive aren't just 'lean', they're interconnected and consider colleagues. In other words, they look left and right, as well as knowing the direction of travel.

2.3 Challenge assumptions

Legacy is not strategy. As we've already demonstrated, most of us are carrying rafts that we cannot see. Over time, businesses become habit machines. The same supplier gets renewed. The same contract rolls over. The same assumptions go untested. 'We've always used them', 'We do *need* it', 'They're the best in market', 'No one else can do it'.

Challenging assumptions isn't about being difficult. It's about being awake, about being switched on. This principle was born from watching millions in spend justified by nothing more than tradition or internal politics.

At the end of the previous century, even the might of NASA messed up royally. NASA lost the $125 million dollar Mars Climate Orbiter because one team (in the UK predictably) had used imperial measurements and the team in the US had failed to perform a software task to convert them to metric.

Everyone just assumed they were speaking the same language. Assumptions like this can hide in plain sight and only show up once it's far too late. Not only should you question assumptions, but you should question them throughout – 'Is what we're assuming here *still the case*?'.

Assumptions can comfort us. They can make a job shorter, easier and less complicated. But in dynamic markets, making them is dangerous. Leadership teams should act like investigative journalists and repeatedly demand answers. What's the source? Is it still credible? What's changed since it was true? This principle invites zero-based thinking: if we started fresh, would we even do it this way today? Would we do it *at all*? What could be done instead?

Organisations that build this into their review cycles uncover surprising inefficiencies and even bigger opportunities. You can't redesign your cost base without challenging the scaffolding that is holding everything up.

2.4 Value before cost

As we explain in detail later, cheapest rarely means best and expensive doesn't guarantee it either. Cheap often, in fact, means hidden cost will follow later. That hidden cost can mean a reduction in quality, an increase in risk or can create work that needs to be done again.

Prudence is not buying at the lowest price. Real value is about quantifying what you *get*, not just what you *pay*. While we feel that procurement teams should be just as incentivised as their sales colleagues for generating profit margin, we accept it can be complicated. Teams that generate a 'win' by switching to cheaper options sometimes only end up spending more money fixing what they broke.

A software license renewal might save £50k upfront but cost you £75k in training and lost productivity. This principle reframes the conversation. Sellers have been able to sell on return on investment (ROI) for years and years. What about the concept of return on spend? ROS, or ROAS, shouldn't just be for advertisers.

Instead of asking 'What's the lowest price we can get?', ask 'What return do we need from this spend?'. This value can include performance, usability, durability, support. It includes internal harmony and external trust. It includes the time you save on internal process management but can subtract the time you waste.

What's cheap to buy is often expensive to own. Imagine you run a hotel. Buying the cheapest fixtures and fittings is sure to increase budgets of ongoing maintenance and replacements. It is also likely to increase customer complaints, which could cost you dearly. A budget price can create premium problems.

Or look at it on another scale entirely. Our 20th-century obsession with cheaper and faster has led to unintended consequences. Whether it's about carbon emissions from companies and vehicles, or microplastics in the environment, the cost of our capitalist largesse will be borne by future generations.

Smart procurement functions lead with outcomes. They run total-cost-of-ownership models. They track post-purchase impact. They talk to users *before* they talk to suppliers.

Value is harder to define, which is why cost so often wins by default. But the best businesses fight for clarity. They understand that aligned, strategic spending is an investment, and investments are judged by returns, not receipts.

2.5 Profit fuels progress

Businesses exist to make money, that's a fact. What each chooses to do with the profits they make can define success and failure. Overspend and overestimate sales, and get hit with a shock – the impact can hurt. Make a healthy profit, but take too much out of the business and invest too little and the sun might shine in the short-term, but it won't be long until the rain sets in.

There's nothing noble about starving yourself either. The trick is to get the balance right and understand that profit isn't just there to line shareholders pockets. Solid profit margins attract investment and enable growth. They enable investment and a greater appetite for risk. Every organisation has a mission. Profit enables you to continue yours.

Teams are often told to do more with less, not to build surplus. But we believe that profit is what gives businesses breathing room. It funds resilience. It allows companies and organisations to have *choice*. It enables you to invest in the organisation, whether R&D, new technology, or staff salaries and incentives, as well as taking out dividends.

In one case we know of, a manufacturer missed a grant renewal because its team was burnt out and under-resourced. In trying to operate too thinly, they ended up with lower margins. In another, a high-growth SME refused to reinvest savings in the business and watched as culture degraded, and their best people jumped ship for better conditions elsewhere. They eventually sold the business for a lower than anticipated value.

> Sara Blakely founded Spanx with $5,000, no investors and a determination to remain independent. Her margins were healthy from day one and she invested her profits back into the business to fund her growth. Staying profitable allowed her to stay independent, eventually enabling her to turn that $5,000 into a billion dollar plus net worth following the sale in 2021. She even used the profit to give her 750 employees $10,000 each and two first-class plane tickets to anywhere in the world. The video you might have seen online doesn't *say* they are return tickets, but we assume so.

Anita Roddick used per profit to drive her purpose. She built her brand around fair-trade and cruelty-free products decades before it was fashionable. Stella McCartney came later, both proving that profit can give principles a platform.

The post-war Marshall Plan of American investment in Europe proved that when you use resources well, you can build a whole new world.

2.6 Sustainability is survival

Being sustainable isn't a cost. Long-term, it's about hedging risk. Sustainability is no longer a laudable ambition, a compliance obligation or a merely a legal one. Being sustainable in the truest sense just means being able to carry on. If you want to still be in business 10, 20 or 30 years from now, you need to ensure your business is sustainable. It's that simple.

While 'Corporate Social Responsibility (CSR)' and more recently 'Environmental, Social and Governance (ESG)' have crept onto corporate agendas, there has always been a feeling – one we have seen far too often – that too many organisations treat sustainability as a compliance obligation, not a cost strategy. Yet time and again, we saw the opposite: energy efficiency reducing bills, better packaging reducing waste, local sourcing improving carbon footprints, the list goes on.

Remember, anything you are paying for people to take off you as part of a waste contract is just that: wastage. Look further up the process to minimise waste in the first place.

Jonas Kjellberg, of Skype fame, talked to us about how to innovate in zeros. A radical approach to efficiency, innovating to zero means applying a critical eye to everything in the business. Do you need it at all? Can you find another way, or a more efficient workaround that means you can eliminate a spend completely? Aligned with overall business purpose, where you can ask yourself – 'Do we really need to buy this *at all?*'.

> Uber, the world's biggest taxi company doesn't own any vehicles and Airbnb reduced cleaning costs to zero by not owning any hotel rooms. Think outside the box and this idea, though it seems radical, can have practical applications. Technology has changed things too. An uptick in online meetings means that fleet and travel costs shrink, replaced by tools that barely trouble the IT budget.

Sustainable choices reduce emissions *and* excess. They eliminate overproduction and avoid fines. They create reputational lift and regulatory headroom. If the spend creates waste, you're buying failure. If it creates resilience, you're buying time.

Sustainable decisions are smart business decisions. The world changes quickly and whether you are still in business 20 years from now will depend on how you behave. As Günther Thallinger – a board member at Allianz in Germany – has warned, there is no future of capitalism without financial services, yet climate-driven risks are fast becoming uninsurable. Act on sustainability with intent and intelligence and it might not just save you some money – it might just save us all.

2.7 Control the cost of change

Change is inevitable. There is nothing you can do to stop it. Think for a second, outside of the usual narrow 'next year's budget' or '5-year plan'. Go for a slightly longer term. Even beyond your tenure, to how your business, the world of work, the world in general might look 50 years from now – perhaps for the sake of your children.

If you go back 50 years, we were all watching TV in black and white. Fifty years before that and we're post WW1 and Spanish-flu, in the middle of the Great Depression and heading inexorably towards WW2. Go back another 100 years before that, we're using candles and bloodletting was a standard medical practice. The world has changed so much since the Industrial Revolution and we forge ahead, without pause for thought. Life changes. Controlling that change is being ahead of the curve. It's either that, or you adapt later, because either way there's nothing you can do to stop it.

One of the things we've observed over the years, is that great ideas fail when you forget to budget for adoption. This principle came from hard-earned experience: seeing brilliant strategies abandoned because no one accounted for training, integration, or allowed enough time for the messages to land. One client implemented a major system overhaul to save money without factoring in the change management process. The staff were revolting (stop sniggering). The savings? Evaporated. Gone.

> Recently, Neil got a new puppy. Although he had factored in the cost of the puppy, the food, the vet bills and insurance, he didn't budget for the sleepless nights or the shredded clothing. This is what change looks like. Not just the single decision that you make to change X for Y, but the inevitable cascade of secondary costs. Without careful planning, what looks like a simple single decision comes with consequences and unanticipated expenses.
>
> Neil doesn't regret getting the puppy for a single second. But once again, he should have considered his own advice and priced in the reality. He did not do enough thinking during the preparation stage. As Abraham Lincoln said, 'If you have 6 hours to cut down a tree, spend the first 4 sharpening the axe.'

After 30 years' experience in suppler management, we have become change management experts. Change costs more than just the thing being changed. New tools require alignment. New suppliers require trust. They require not just learning new systems or processes but also unlearning old ones. Humans react and require management to accept, rather than resist changes. Yet another element that requires advance planning and the proper acknowledgement of the associated costs.

Smart businesses bake in the *real* cost of transition. They scope it up front. They build in time for habits to shift. They fund communication, advocates and champions, not just software upgrades. When it comes to change and transformation, you must expect friction. It is not a failure; it is an inevitability and, therefore, it's a cost line. Treat it that way.

2.8 Spend to strengthen

As any weight watcher will tell you, cutting muscle rather than fat, is not a great result. At first, some of the most impactful spending we've seen looked inefficient. A client kept funding internal analytics, even as outsourcing seemed cheaper. Years later, that team had saved millions by unlocking cross-functional insights. Another invested heavily in learning and development, and hugely reduced attrition, thereby reducing recruitment costs.

When was the last time you had a gym membership? Did you go regularly? Why did you end it? As most of us know, gyms sell memberships to more people than could ever fit inside. They rely on most of us not showing up. It's a subscription service guaranteeing smugness for some and guilt for others. For some, that spend is a surface-level change without effect.

By contrast, as we will see with Milo of Craton later, building muscle is a process. Both might make you feel better about yourself (at least for a time), but only one of these delivers results. One is a transaction; the other is a transformation. Nobody applauds you for attending first-aid training, but those plaudits soon come when that training saves a life. Training, systems and tools can seem like an unnecessary expense – until they pay dividends.

If we aim to teach you anything, it's that not all pricing is equal. Some spending weakens you. Some spending fortifies you. What you need is the wisdom to know the difference.

This principle says: don't mistake economy for strength. Spend where it builds resilience, capability or culture. Trim where it doesn't. Contrary to what some people might try and tell you, you can't cost-cut your way to competitive advantage. But you can *invest* toward it.

2.9 Build for visibility

If you can't see it, you can't control it. And if you can't explain it, you can't improve it. The number of clients we've seen blindsided by auto-renewals, missed thresholds, or undocumented agreements is not a small number. Not a small percentage even. Visibility is the first line of defence against waste and the launchpad for improvement.

Most consulting firms are engaged by clients to help with strategy, or to fix a known problem. There is a fire, an email is sent and along come the management consultants with their bucket of water and hose. Many organisations do not believe they have a problem with costs or, if they do, do not believe that the gains that can be made outweigh the perceived hassle of fixing them.

Cost management consultants are rarely called in because a client recognises that things are on fire. Usually, our job is to get them to smell the smoke. Trying to change that mindset to one that understands the potential gains to be made by focusing here is part of the purpose of this book.

> We all know the feeling of looking in a well-stocked cupboard or fridge and complaining that we can't find anything to eat. If not us, our teenagers for sure. Now imagine what that looks like when you're looking at your store, your warehouse, your goods in transit inbound and out. Too often, people cannot see what they are looking at. Tracking inventory is a requirement, but tracking cost can get lost.
>
> Without visibility, abundance is confusion. There's a reason we can't see the wood for the trees. Cost works in the same way – if you can't see them, you can't manage them meaningfully. To *Build for Visibility* means consciously designing data, dashboards and reporting into your purchasing and supplier selection decisions.

The fix is always the same: make costs visible. Especially the ones that can slip through the net. Use dashboards. Build spending reviews into performance rhythms. Track savings but also track *losses prevented*.

Visibility empowers better questions. It also shares the burden. If only procurement can see spend, only procurement can fix it. If everyone can, accountability is distributed. You don't need perfect reporting. You need consistent sightlines. What you are spending is not some unknowable mystery. Don't treat it like one.

2.10 Enough is a strategy

As we've explained, spending less isn't always wise. Spending just enough is the art.

This final principle challenges the cultural assumption that more is always better. More coverage. More features. More stock. More sales. More staff. More growth. More hassle?

The reality is many businesses drown in excess. They over-insure. Over-stock. Over-spec. It looks like safety precautions, but it's waste. Worse still, it creates friction: too much choice, too much inventory, too many moving parts can cause decision paralysis.

Have you ever packed for a two-day business trip and packed five sets of underwear? What do we think is going to happen? When we do this, we're not responding to logic, we're responding to anxiety. *Enough* means deciding what's sufficient and resisting the urge to overcompensate for nebulous reasons. You're – presumably, you might be reading this in bed – already wearing one pair, so pack two more and maybe one for luck in future.

Overpreparing for the *wrong* risk distracts you from what really matters. It's probably more important to review your presentation again than it is to fret about your underwear.

This principle applied as we watched a client cut back its software stack by 40%, with zero impact on operations, as well as generating a major gain in usability. Sufficient is not stingy. It's strategic. It says: 'We will define what's sufficient and hold ourselves to it'. Review whether what you have is necessary. Really necessary.

More is often mistaken for better; companies as diverse as Toyota and Patagonia have grown intentionally, not endlessly. Not every business wants to join the FAANG club. It's ok to limit growth and ambition if that is what suits you. Some people want to build big, and others want to build meaning. Some want an empire; some are happy with a village. Some want to know the name of every employee; some can't remember how many countries they are in.

Enough is a Strategy is designed to challenge the default modern assumption that scale is success. It is not restraint for its own sake. It's discipline. It's knowing where growth stops creating value.

chapter 3

Executive concerns

3.1 What keeps you up at night?

The same core anxieties keep senior leaders awake at night: shrinking margins and exposure to unexpected costs. Many organisations have blind spots because they confuse process compliance with genuine control.

Every senior executive understands pressure. You're responsible for growth, people, cashflow, compliance and reputation – all at the same time. The decisions you make affect dozens, hundreds, even thousands of people. Time is precious. There is never enough of it. To ensure that your responsibilities as a director are met, and to protect the interests of your workforce, the best thing to do is try and ensure the long-term sustainability and growth of the business. Always try to make decisions with this in mind.

Away from responsibilities for your human capital and culture, the other main executive concerns are for areas that also help to create this long-term sustainability.

This is a combination of:

- Managing financial performance and cash flow
- Managing risk and compliance
- Setting the strategic vision for the business
- Driving growth
- Ensuring operational efficiency

- Delivering innovation
- Managing partner relationships
- Ensuring the business addresses the issues associated with climate change, sustainability, and social responsibility.

While that's quite a list, there is also the simple way of looking at financial health and growth. Sell more to grow and spend less to maximise profit. Selling more requires setting up sales teams and systems, giving them the clear value propositions to sell, creating and executing marketing plans, developing more competitive products, employing a pricing strategy, delivering more training and myriad other activities, all with a cost attached.

Controlling the financial performance of cashflow is the lifeblood of the business. This is vital for everything else to work. Managing risk and compliance ensures that there are no painful and/or expensive surprises in your future. Being on top of efficiency and innovation means you are always using the right things and doing the right things. Steering your relationships with the supply chain ensures that raw materials reach your business and allow it to operate. Addressing the social, economic and environmental responsibilities of your business enables you to have the right people on board and a sustainable future.

In a market economy, profit functions as an exceptionally helpful signal to the market. Companies that are consistently more profitable have opportunities that others do not: to attract and retain the best talent, to invest in the best research & development and in new production machines or advertising. In these companies, the money they generate is further reinforced by the fact that it is also they who can most easily attract funding from investors and banks, since they prefer to invest their money and manage their risk with more profitable companies.

In business, as in life, having money makes it far easier to make more. Good financial results today have the advantage of making it easier to obtain even better financial results in the future. To make better decisions companies should view who is being incentivised where, and for what, in terms of the long-term health of the company.

There are thousands of books, videos, courses, systems and countless sales 'gurus' telling us all how to sell more and sell better. Sales and marketing topics have historically been very popular, and that industry itself is worth billions, before we even get to the dollars spent on marketing and advertising, which is also all designed to drive more sales. We can always feel we can sell more, but don't appear to believe with anything like the same weight, that we can also spend less, with zero other impact.

Having a large sales team without properly focussing on cost is like building a skyscraper with shallow foundations. It might look impressive, but it might not stay standing for long.

Our aim in this book is to help organisations to understand that you can continue to be excellent for your customers – still be recognisably 'you' – and continue to serve your clients at the highest level and to provide employment for your staff, while being more focused on cost management, as well as sales.

Profit isn't just about growth and sales. It's about the gap between revenues and costs. Focus on one side of the equation and you'll get what you've always got. But if you can *Spend with Purpose* as well, smarter, more sustainable profits become possible.

Smarter spending is not about slashing. It means aligning every pound, dollar or euro you spend with your goals. Great executives design systems that eliminate waste, reinforce purpose and *strengthen* for a sustainable future.

3.2 A comfortable cushion means better sleep

So how do you sleep better? Clarity is more than operational hygiene; it is emotional security for leaders. When you can see and understand where your money is going, the anxiety of uncertainty eases.

When a financial crisis hits a household, a company, or a country, the same realisation often follows. For too long, we've spent too much and saved too little. The pain lands hardest on those without a financial cushion. Conversely, the well-prepared can prosper.

If disaster hits, governments have more levers to pull. For businesses and individuals, the only real solution is simple – earn more, spend less and do both before the next storm hits. Just like the more far-sighted countries, good companies do not have major problems even in times of crisis. Many even grow, either by taking advantage of the general reduction in resources, by buying national or foreign competitors or by benefiting from the bankruptcy of lesser competitors.

So, while many companies are just busy surviving, others are already preparing for the future and trying now to create the cushions that will allow them to survive the next crisis, whenever it may come. Strong companies are working to become even stronger. They do so by paying attention to opportunities on both sides of the Income Statement.

Each pound or dollar reduced in costs, if it guarantees no negative effects on the quality of the goods or services provided by the company, is one more available to build the protective cushion, whatever its form.

Anyone who has had financial difficulties at some point in their life knows that you sleep better without worries than with them. Knowing this, it will always be healthier to have built a comfortable financial cushion to continue sleeping well, even in turbulent times.

It is also worth remembering that we can get by with less than we think. As the pandemic in 2020 taught us, sacred cows can sometimes be slaughtered after all. When considering the safety and comfort you need, assess the risk – alongside your insurance advisers – you are prepared to take. Real security doesn't come from endless efforts at optimisation, but sometimes, from the confidence that what you already have is enough.

Smarter spending is not just financial, but emotional too. It's about knowing you've built something strong enough to stand the waves when they break. That kind of resilience is worth investing in – it's what helps you sleep at night.

chapter 4

Obstacles to progress

4.1 What process management can learn from competitive eating

Adding more resources, steps or effort does not guarantee better results, it often creates waste and confusion. Organisations default to complexity because it feels safer or more impressive, but real value usually comes from simplification.

Open your mind, and you can learn clever things in surprising places. Let us give you an example, by asking a question. What's the silliest sport in the world? Opinions will vary. For some, it's football – 22 millionaires chasing a ball round while spending half their time rolling on the floor. For others it might be NASCAR, the very definition of going round in circles.

Our vote goes to competitive eating. For those unfamiliar with the concept, competitive eating consists of eating as much as you possibly can, during a limited time and it is surprisingly big business. Devotees pack into live events – usually in the USA & Japan – in their thousands, and large events are broadcast live on sports channels and watched by millions.

At the turn of this century, a single athlete transformed the landscape of this sport and there is a lesson in the approach he took. In 2001, Takeru Kobayashi lived with his girlfriend in Sapporo, Japan, working low-wage jobs, in enough debt to be behind on the rent and eating by candlelight after being cut off for non-payment of bills by the power company.

For reasons more of desperation than anything tangible, Kobayashi's girlfriend put his name up for a local competitive eating event with a cash prize. Kobayashi did not look like a typical competitive eater. He was slim and short. To the surprise of all participants – including himself – Kobayashi took top prize that day. The story could easily have stopped there.

Kobayashi, however, decided he had a talent and wanted to see how far he could take it. He decided to enter the most famous competitive eating event in the world: Nathan's Famous Hot Dog Eating Contest. Held each 4 July since 1972 in Coney Island, New York, the event was broadcasted live through ESPN and reached millions of viewers.

Kobayashi knew he did not have the expected build for the sport. To compete at an internationally serious level, he decided he had to think and act differently to stand a chance. Most competitors ate the hot dog the way we all do. Start from one end, chewing and swallowing, perhaps drinking some water to help wash it down, then on to the next.

Kobayashi deconstructed the process, experimented and timed different ways to do it, until he settled on quite a different form. The Kobayashi method involved separating the sausage from the bun, breaking both in half, then putting the pieces of sausage in his mouth and chewing while dipping the bread in the water. He then used the wet bun to help push down the sausage, even as his hands were already preparing the next dog. Kobayashi practised until he had perfected the process.

Come the day of the event, he took to the stage in front of an enthusiastic crowd, behind a large table filled with hot dogs. Behind each competitor, promo staff held the boards signalling how many hot dogs each competitor had eaten. Between them and the table sat the stars of the show, a line of big heavy eating athletes.

Among them, all 58 kg of Kobayashi.

To the crowd, the newcomer did not look like one of the favourites. Not even in the same league. The competitors had 12 minutes to eat as many hot dogs as they could. In the 30 years that the competition had taken place, the winner was usually able to consume around 20 hot dogs, with 25 being the record.

Once the competition started, Kobayashi's strange technique quickly drew the attention of both crowd and TV audience. Within minutes, the difference in the numbers achieved by him and all the other competitors was starting to become evident. The promo girl standing behind him ran out of numbers on her board and had to start writing it down using a marker pen.

When the 12 minutes were over and the bell rang, Kobayashi had eaten 50 hot dogs, doubling the previous record. There was total astonishment.

Imagine someone running 100 metres in just five seconds. Unbelievable. Kobayashi had changed the landscape of competitive eating forever, in just 12 minutes.

Now known as 'The Tsunami', Kobayashi dominated the sport for 6 years and is arguably still it's most famous star. You may never have heard of him before now, but he is to competitive eating what Michael Jordan is to basketball or Tiger Woods is to golf. He makes his very good living from advertising and personal appearances.

Was he just a genetic freak? We know the tale of Michael Phelps' unique lung capacity. Was this person who doubled the record a phenomenon? He was not. Armed with the methods and insights Kobayashi had developed, other competitors – including similarly slight young men and women – eventually started beating his performances.

Today, the record stands at 75 hot dogs in 12 minutes. Completely unthinkable until Kobayashi.

To be clear, we do not advocate for entering the competitive eating arena; in fact, we believe that watching a couple of videos should be more than enough for most people. But as unlikely as it sounds, Kobayashi's story offers a near perfect blueprint for cost transformation.

Here are four lessons that apply beyond the buffet:

1 ***Challenge Assumptions*: everything can be improved, even when we do not believe it can be.** More than that, everything is improvable, *especially* when we think it cannot be. Before Kobayashi broke into the competitive eating arena, everyone – competitors, organisers, spectators – believed that substantial improvements from the number 25 were unlikely, so even if the record were to be broken, it would be by only one or two hot dogs more. Everyone was so convinced by the story they told themselves, that seeing another way seemed completely impossible. Now, knowing the record is 75, eating 25 in 12 minutes seems almost do-able. See you back after lunch!

2 ***Spend to Strengthen*: new methods outperform old ones.** Had he opted for the traditional way of doing things, Kobayashi would never have crushed the record. He managed to develop his own new technique, by hard working at it. Working alone is often not practical, and in most business areas, developing genuine expertise takes many years. If you do not have the specialist know-how in a certain area, do not hesitate to ask for help from someone who does. Ignorance is expensive. A will to try new things, coupled with expertise and know-how, can vastly outperform historical performance.

3 *See the Whole System*: **deconstructing the full task** was key to Kobayashi's development of the new method. He realised he had three parts (bun, sausage, water) he could separate (the bun from the sausage), break (both the bun and the sausage) or combine (the bun with water), to achieve the best overall result. Likewise, to achieve the global purpose of getting our goods to our clients in pristine conditions, we can opt for many combinations of packaging materials, separating, breaking or combining various materials to achieve the optimal result.
4 *Control the Cost of Change*: **deliberate practice leads to improved results.** It was not enough for Kobayashi to develop his new method. He had to train repeatedly, perfecting it as he went along. The same applies to change management, the more you practice and absorb the mindset, the better you will become.

Incorporating continuous improvement, being willing to try radically new things, demonstrating the correct know-how, questioning all processes and adopting a cost reduction mindset, are of the utmost importance. So is time: the time to analyse, to study, to practice. We understand time is maybe the most valuable asset we all have. It seems to continuously run out, until the inevitable day it runs out completely.

The most important question may be to what priorities should we devote our time, and that is why we devoted the chapter after next solely to it. We should track time, with as much scrutiny as we attach to money and resources.

Often, wasted time spent by employees has a knock-on effect to profitability. *'Building for Visibility'* doesn't just mean create dashboards to track supplier data: it is about providing clarity of purpose for everyone. How people spend their time, planning, executing – and creating new systems or applications like our friend Kobayashi – is just as important as how they spend money.

Finally, consider those 50 years of minimal, incremental improvements. How much time passed with everyone assuming minimal, incremental improvements were all that could be hoped for? What a waste. Imagine if that level of compounded improvement has been reached earlier. Where would they be today? Another reason why focusing on these kinds of initiatives should have started yesterday, not on a tomorrow that never comes.

Competitive eating may still be the daftest sport in the world. But it has still provided us with valuable lessons. Breakthroughs don't come by doing more of the same, but from thinking differently. Just ask the man who doubled the record.

4.2 Knowledge really is power

Incomplete or outdated information quietly destroys margin. Mistakes come not from bad intentions but from relying on bad data. Clarity and transparency are the bedrock of smarter spending. Question the accuracy of reports that look comforting on the surface.

We all have our own areas of expertise. Take the two of us for example. Pedro is a solid ultra-marathon runner and understands the way in which he needs to take care of his body to perform at its best. Neil on the other hand is confident in his general knowledge across a range of subjects – just sometimes *too* confident.

The two authors of this book share areas of knowledge: for example, business, sales and procurement. They also share some areas of ignorance. Not knowing too much about cars has cost them both over the years. No doubt the total is in the thousands of euros so far.

For anyone that knows their own job better than the person they are speaking to, it is easy to determine with a couple of questions the level of knowledge in their area of expertise that the person in front of them possesses. If that is a supplier salesperson and it becomes plain to them that their buyers' knowledge level is low, it presents a clear opportunity to increase their profit margin.

Not everybody takes those opportunities, but many do. Some even do so by the kinds of substantial amounts that are unethical. We are sure that, unless you happen to be an expert not only in mechanics, but also in plumbing, electricity, dentistry, telecommunications, law and many other fields of expertise, you will have overpaid for materials and services at work and at home.

Although we have also been taken advantage of, many times, we try to refrain from blaming the seller, unless they were dishonest – like the mechanic who charged for a new part, having installed an old one. Making the most out of the opportunities we are presented with is something most people are wired to do.

What is true when it happens to us in person is also true in business. In procurement, ignorance can be very expensive. No one really likes to think of themselves as dishonest or bad. When salespeople see an opportunity to profit from a lack of detailed knowledge on your part, they rationalise that we, on the receiving end, were paying for our ongoing business education, albeit unknowingly. Suppliers also have kids to feed.

A lack of knowledge is one of the most important obstacles to saving money, both at home and in your business. It is impractical and uneconomical to have inside your company people with expertise in all 40+ of the overhead cost areas that you buy from. A metalworks producer will have staff with deep knowledge of different metals – their composition, dimensions and uses. They will know how to buy metals at a world-class level. It is unlikely they have the same kind of deep expertise in the purchase of insurance, or telecoms, or IT, or packaging. Yet many companies assume that because they excel at one topic, they excel in all of them.

As that reliable source of great quotes Mark Twain once put it, *'It's not what you don't know that gets you into trouble. It is what you know for sure that just ain't so.'*

Worse than ignorance is assuming you know the subject and being wrong. However, if you recognise you are not an expert, you may search for more information or for independent and unbiased advice. If you believe you already hold all the answers, you will stick more steadfastly to your argument, independent of how right or wrong you may be.

The best way to prevent the lack of know-how from harming your cost reduction strategies is to adopt an 'I need to know more' attitude. Apply it to everything, even the matters you take for granted. Better still, especially those. A business that does not understand its spending landscape is flying blind. Visibility gives insight, and insights give you strategic leverage. Make sure you understand interdependencies across the supply chain, and the potential organisational impact.

You wouldn't diagnose your own root canal. Don't make six-figure spending decisions without expert insight. The smartest businesses, like the smartest people, don't pretend to know everything. They know their limits, and they know when to ask for help.

4.3 You have time – if you spend it carefully

Time is like money, a resource that can be wasted or invested. When organisations say they lack time to review costs properly, it often means they have not prioritised it. Allocate time towards activities that improve profitability and resilience.

Nobody ever thinks they have enough time. But is it true? Numerous studies show that boredom is the required precursor to creativity. Our brains need to be relaxed to allow new connections and ideas to form. How far back do you have to go, do you think, to find those idyllic years when you had the time to get bored? Childhood?

Nowadays, we are all bombarded with requests from all angles in myriad ways, which seem only to increase. We have developed an extraordinary range of productivity tools: word processing, unbelievably quick computers, the internet, email and messaging apps like Slack or Teams, all delivered instantly via laptops, smartphones and tablets. But do we really have any more time available than we used to?

While those productivity tools have multiplied, so too the number of requests we are exposed to has increased exponentially, sucking away our attention and focus. The ceaseless monotony is not only draining but also disheartening, as it underscores the loss of our most precious and irreplaceable resource.

Of course, time can be a fluid concept. We all have the same number of hours in a day, but if an important client calls with a serious problem, or our child's school calls, then suddenly, we can 'magic up' the time to solve these problems. So, if we agree that we can fit in time to perform tasks that we were not expecting, then we can conclude that this time must somehow *always* have *been available*.

We will continue to find time in the future to fit in new unexpected tasks or emergencies, meaning we must also have time available right now – even if we cannot necessarily see it. There are always new ideas, new products and new projects underway. The question in business, as in our private lives, is what is the best way to spend our time?

According to Jonathan Ive, one of Steve Jobs' greatest qualities was focus. Not his ability to switch that focus on during a meeting, or on a Monday morning, but to be laser-focused, always, on the outcome. Is the time I am spending on this contributing to the overall mission and goal? That should be the focus of everyone working in business.

On that basis, it is easy to understand why many believe that the best way to spend their time inside the business is to focus on how to increase sales. We live, after all, in a world predicated on economic growth.

We know that CEOs spend more time dedicated to the sales function of the business than they do on costs. In fact (according to Harvard Business School), the average CEO spends just 1% of their time with suppliers, despite spend with suppliers typically accounting for almost half of their turnover. In some ways, this is understandable, since increases in sales are more visible markers of success and growth. However, in other ways, this focus on sales, rather than on the costs is madness, given the cost of sales and the benefits of savings and the paucity of time.

We mostly feel that time is slipping through our fingers, because we fail to manage it effectively – even at work, even with all our productivity tools. We don't tend to mismanage time because we are lazy, but because we are unclear. Until you know what matters most, everything can be equally urgent and equally overwhelming.

And then there is human nature to factor in. No matter how accomplished we are, we sometimes make whatever is the easiest decision. Exercise or read? Volunteer or watch TV? Start a cost reduction project or just let things stand and believe the status quo is as good as it gets?

If you are reading this book, there is a high probability that your status quo is not good enough, if you can now begin to smell improvements. It's likely that:

(a) you are dynamic and have a lot of projects going on
(b) you are committed to self-improvement, both on a personal and company level
(c) you sometimes postpone stuff, either to 'later' or to 'never'

If both (a) and (b) are true (and if you have read this far, we are willing to bet they are), then you will be a person who wants to apply your time in the most productive way. As we have demonstrated, it is not always clear what that path is. Statement (c) is always true for everyone, because you are human, and we all postpone one thing or another.

Investing time in cutting costs usually yields excellent returns. *'Seeing the Whole System'* includes thinking from the suppliers' perspective, creating dashboards and building visibility – not just in important areas, but across the enterprise. While you're using Pareto to focus on the 80%, you could be amazed at what leaks from the 20.

When something is that highly productive, do not postpone or delay it. We all know that you will never have enough time to do everything you want to. Use this lesson. Time is not your enemy; indecision is. Don't say 'I don't have time'. Say 'it's not a priority' and sit with how that feels. If it doesn't feel good, do something about it. Anything else is more time wasted.

4.4 Build a cost-conscious culture

Lasting improvements are cultural, not procedural. Rules and policies alone won't work if teams don't feel ownership over spending decisions. A cost-conscious culture grows through transparency, regular dialogue and visible leadership commitment.

Sales directors and their teams are undoubtedly important (if often a drain on company expense accounts!), but when was the last time you held a savings competition or took the 'best savers' out to lunch, for a slap-up dinner, or away for a conference? We bet never. Buyers are often independent, unrelated to one another, heads of different departments – sometimes very different departments.

What logic is there in assuming that as well as being head of their departments, they can also assume responsibility for ensuring optimal purchasing across all their areas of responsibilities? Is that not a huge job – at least at times – in itself? Are they not subject matter experts in Finance, HR, Marketing and the like, as opposed to being buying experts?

Your IT director is where they are due to technical knowledge and the experience of gaining management skills. Their job is to run all aspects of your IT, usually including photocopiers, mobile phones, specifying hardware and software licensing and requirements, as well as managing a team of developers, a helpdesk, outside partner relationships, the website and, finally, just the small matter of all your essential cyber security. They are already running fast. Is it either fair or realistic to expect them to ace all the procurement and optimise the budget as well? What percentage of their time do even they spend with their suppliers, and running RFx? 5%? 1%?

Some of your employees, let's be frank, don't care anyway. It is not their money they are spending, and some will always be a bit more 'fast and loose' with company cash than they are with their own. That said, creating a cost-conscious culture is mostly a matter of acknowledging that there is a problem – and a little time and application.

We know that businesses have cost in all sorts of areas, and they are often chaotic, complex, seasonal, across multiple locations and managed by myriad departments and budget holders. There are also often plenty of other staff authorised to make smaller orders. It is no wonder that sometimes it can seem like unpicking all of that and having it run like clockwork is a daunting prospect.

There are complex areas like fleet and logistics, where decisions around long-term planning like financing and how to buy, as well as what to buy and from whom, require deeper thinking around the consequences and risk. However, there are also some quick wins and gains to be made in most other areas.

It does not need to feel like pushing water uphill to manage it all efficiently either. In fact, believe it or not, when installing a more cost-conscious culture amongst your employees, half the battle is just talking about it. Like so many things, this is really a problem of communication.

Many organisations proudly describe themselves as 'sales-led', and that's a great thing. It is good to have an effort to create a culture at all. Unless it's toxic. To have one focussed on growth and driving success, especially one where the success is shared and staff feel empowered, rewarded and incentivised is fantastic.

Most organisations prioritise savings when they are forced to. For some, by then, it's too late. The definition of madness is doing the same thing over again and expecting a different result. Yet time and again we see organisations making the same mistakes.

Company directors carry dual responsibilities. Protect the people and protect the business. That means fostering a fair, inclusive workplace and ensuring its long-term financial health to reward staff and shareholders. Ensuring that the company is profitable, cash safe and geared for long-term sustainability also means looking after those pennies, so that the pounds look after themselves.

Carry on waving wads of cash at your successful salespeople and keep them happy but remember it's the cost of everything you buy that determines the *profit gap* between turnover and cost of sales. They have their own mantra – ABC: Always Be Closing. But every cost-conscious company should Always Be Counting. If you prefer something shorter, just remember to mind the gap.

4.5 When you don't have the money, use the difficulty

View scarcity as a catalyst for innovation rather than an excuse to do nothing. Constraints can clarify priorities and drive more creative solutions. Spending less does not have to mean doing less; it can mean doing more of what matters most.

Sometimes, making improvements can be expensive. One of the main obstacles for companies to grow is having the financial wherewithal to be able to invest and make that leap. Sometimes it might be machinery that will significantly increase productivity but has a high initial cost. Other times it will be wanting to add more human resources that can only be attracted by higher salaries than those for which there is current capacity to pay.

It's paradoxical: to be able to earn more money, we first must have more money. A company with excellent financial capacity will be able to invest more quickly in means that allow it to grow or optimise its business than another whose financing capacity is exhausted.

Regardless of where you are between these two extremes, everyone weighs up the risks and benefits of each potential investment for their business. There is another advantage for financially healthier companies too. If an investment goes wrong, it is unlikely to be as damaging as it would be to a business in a poor position, for whom it can be fatal.

Growth always has a cost but the most successful companies budget for it rather than resist reality. But if you don't have the money, what else can you do?

Michael Caine said in an interview that during his early career as a theatre actor, he was involved in an improvisation in which another couple were arguing, and he had to enter their room from behind a stage door. As the couple's improvised row continued and became physical, a chair from the room wedged itself against the door Caine was supposed to come through.

He stood still, not knowing how to proceed. The play's director shouted at him 'use the difficulty! If it's a comedy, fall over it, if it's a drama, pick it up and smash it!'. For Caine, it was a revelatory moment. What he realised was that 'using the difficulty' was applicable to everything, not just the stage.

He says his family and those around him now well know that, when something bad happens, you must think about how to use the difficulty. There is nothing that happens that you cannot turn around. If you can do that, even one percent to your advantage, you're ahead. You didn't let it get you down.

So how can we use the difficulty caused by a lack of money to invest? The answer is naturally more complex than that available to companies that can just write a cheque. It will require imagination and analytical skills. The more you have of both, the better the solutions you will create.

Successful companies can become complacent and get used to just throwing money at a problem. Think of that like always taking the elevator, instead of the stairs. Those of us forced to walk know that it is probably healthier and better for us in the long-term.

The most obvious ways around things with less cash are also, of course, financial. Solutions for business are increasingly abundant and can be complex. You can turn to credit, leasing or renting, for example. You can appeal to investors but there are other ways to climb the stairs.

Process improvement alternatives may be more effective. When resources are tight, better questions matter more.

Consider asking:

- Are there other ways to achieve the same results?
- Can we generate the required resources elsewhere in the company?
- What level of results can we realistically create?

Whatever the questions may be, you can find answers. You can use ingenuity to design simpler machines, or create adaptations to existing efforts that are more efficient yet achieve similar results. You might find that selling some inventory, or an asset that is not very useful or not strategic to retain can finance the new project. You may find savings in other cost areas of the company, which generate the money needed.

For Michael Caine and his family, using the difficulty became a mantra. That said, he agreed in the same interview that avoiding these issues altogether is the better position to be in. The way to make that happen is proactively. Using the difficulties that come your way as opportunities to innovate and improve, to collaborate and problem-solve, is a far better way than, for example, accepting an unwanted change and simply working around it as part of the status quo. Problems you ignore become the rafts that mean you carry extra weight. Problems solved proactively build the foundations for a stronger business: don't wait and get stuck behind the door.

4.6 Escape the budget prison

While budgets are necessary, they often become rigid cages that block smarter decisions. Annual targets can create perverse incentives, like manipulating numbers to look good on paper. Budgets are tools, not commandments, so maintain flexibility to seize opportunities and adjust course when reality changes.

In most large organisations, people live and die by the budget. It seems half the year is spent forecasting next year's numbers. These meetings and negotiations go on year on year. When the budget is finally concluded and distributed, it becomes written in stone.

When the new budget year begins, much of it is spent comparing the ensuing reality with the forecast. This is budgeting as religion, not reason. '*Spend with Purpose*' reminds us that the point is not to adhere to the plan, but to advance the mission. Ask yourself, 'Does each line item on our budget truly serve our strategic goals, or do they persist out of tradition?'. Without purpose, the annual budget ritual can feel pointless.

Budgets are extremely useful management tools, allowing some measure of control over both the future and the past. They help to set goals and expectations. They serve to measure and reward reliable performance. Managing cashflow appropriately allows funds to be available when needed. We are not advocating for an end to budgeting; however, detailing the many advantages budgets bring to an organisation is also futile here. They are widely used because they provide great value.

Our contention is simply that they can be a prison. A constraint. A way of blinkering thought and vision to see only the straight and narrow, thus disallowing more creative solutions. Beyond the time and resources taken and the repetitive revisions, 'sticking to' the budget, by its very nature, can create boundaries to sometimes more worthwhile thoughts and actions. Over the years, we have heard a range of stories companies tell themselves and assumptions they make, that can be limiting.

'If it is not in the annual plan, we're not going to prioritise it.'

Not planning for longer than a year is obviously total madness, yet it happens all the time. Long-term planning is exceedingly rare. Most organisations plan for a year at a time, and may have a strategic vision of a five- or ten-year plan. But many lack the long-term vision that is essential to build a truly sustainable plan. Most organisations do not maximise their growth until well after the first 5 years of operations, but almost all plan in 1–5-year cycles. But the world was very different 40 years ago, and 40 years before that, and will be very different again in another 40, and another.

Elon Musk had a vision to put a human being on Mars by 2025. Given that 2025 has been and gone and his attention has been somewhat… divided, it's clear this deadline was always more about ambition than certainty, but it is noteworthy that he said this as recently as 2016. Even the 'visionary' was looking less than a decade ahead.

- However long you plan for, make sure you are not *too* beholden to your budgets. It stifles innovation and creativity.
- Work out what your long-term plans are and work each year to build towards them, instead of working 1 or 2 to 3 years at a time.

We've also heard people say:

'If the goal is a 5% growth, there is no point in growing 10%, as the following year would be even harder to beat', or 'If the goal is 5% saving, there is no point in saving 10%, as the following year would be even harder to beat.'

Where do you start with this kind of magical thinking? We will deal with these both together. Both are ridiculous positions that professionals somehow manage to talk themselves into on an annual basis.

Deliberately limiting your own performance to hit some arbitrary figure is obviously counter-intuitive, yet it happens all the time. This is budgeting as caution. *Challenge Assumptions* urges us to think, 'Is our growth target really a goal, or is it a ceiling we've mistaken for a virtue?'. There may be *more* opportunity next year, not less, so why limit?

> *'I closed a big deal in November, but it was shipped in February. My goal for last years' sales came up short, but next year's budget is now higher, having already included the big boost in February.'*

This is one we see a lot. The unfairness of it all. You can hear the complaints from the sales teams already. A double-whammy this one, meaning both that the salesperson misses their target – and therefore their bonus – for this year and now also has a hell of a job to reach a larger target next year.

Obvious anomalies like large, one-off unrepeating invoices can sometimes be understood, or explained away, or accommodated in a budget. But arbitrary lines drawn in the sand can result in both an unsatisfied and demotivated sales force, leaving an organisation even less likely to reach even higher targets next year.

Rid yourself of your adherence to the 'year-end' and 'new financial year' and make decisions that make sense for your teams and your business and not just because they fit with the budget.

> *'This is a great investment now, but it will have to wait for next years' budget.'*

Why? If this is a great idea now, why lose time? This is where the *Controlling the Cost of Change* matters. Delaying has a price. Not just financially, but *competitively*. Every month you remain indecisive hands advantage to your rivals.

The arbitrary line drawn in the sand can cause businesses to make poor decisions, or delay investing in resources, research or materials that can pay a future dividend, because 'it is not in the budget'. The delay can be terminal. We know of several businesses which lost huge advantages by delaying investment in new production facilities, thus allowing their rivals to invest more quickly and gain market share, because they were more flexible and more agile in their thinking.

You see this behaviour a lot in 'start-up' environments, where product and technical development going faster or slower than planned can lead lean and agile organisations to (need to) re-budget on a quarterly, or even a monthly basis.

It is a little scary flying by the seat of your pants, but it can deliver huge rewards.

Other 'inmate' behaviours

The budget prison can also lead to either borderline, or even clearly unethical behaviour, like asking suppliers to invoice sooner or postponing client billings, when there is an end-of-year surplus, or the other way around when it comes up short.

In a large multinational we know, whenever the year-end results where short but not too far away, it was customary practice for years to ship unordered goods on the last day of the fiscal year, so goals would be met, and bonuses collected. When the client then returned the goods that they had not ordered, the refund / loss was posted in the following years' accounts. Like in a real prison, being locked in the budget prison too long can send a person mad and they – and in the end entire companies – can make uncharacteristic decisions.

The impact of the budget prison in cost reduction programmes

Sometimes markets go haywire, either up or down, and it is unfair to judge performance by numbers created many months back, when market conditions could have been quite different. If the plastics market is up by 50%, the prices of all related products will also rise. In our experience the art is then in limiting the percentage you get hit with.

Similarly, there is little merit in lowering costs when markets go down. Solving the markets problem may be done by using indices that get reviewed periodically. We can agree that metal is a significant cost for a company that produces metallic furniture, but raw material increases can be difficult to immediately pass on to customers. A year-long budget could be done assuming a certain market price, but each month, subsequent budgets would get hit with the reality of the market input.

Under these circumstances, if the procurement team were buying better relative to the market, it would make sense for them to be rewarded because of losses prevented. This can create of course its own set of problems, as budgeting is more complex and the end target (usually EBITDA (earnings before interest, taxes, depreciation and amortisation) or similar) is a moving one, but it would certainly be fairer. While salespeople are awarded routinely, we rarely see procurement departments earn bonuses related to savings.

If an organisation has a goal to reduce operating costs by 5%, that will be the number in the head of the staff. They will consider the job complete if that number has been achieved. But sometimes, as we know from experience, far more can be possible. Businesses willing to think beyond the brief, and ask better questions, can reduce costs by 50% or more in some areas. In others, they can even cut cost out altogether, or better still, turn them into a cost centre. We can think of several examples of clients paying to have materials removed as waste that can be sold for profit.

None of this will even enter the realm of possibilities of any organisation with a fixed 5% target, so results like that could never be achieved. That's why *Enough is a Strategy* also matters. We are obsessed with rounded numbers and annual targets can strangle imagination. Sometimes the optimal is exponential, not just linear. We should *Challenge Assumptions* that saving a percentage here or there is all that is possible. Instead of fretting over whether you'll hit the target, look deeper at what the goals are. Usually, the biggest gains to be made are by asking whether your targets are even worth hitting.

Your business is evolving all the time, not once a year. Smart leaders understand that budget reform is emotional as much as technical. People resist change when they don't see the ramp between now and next. On the other hand, it can happen that the suppliers are so stretched that even a 1% reduction can be impossible to get, and yet they will be pushed to the 5% mark, sometimes causing cracks in the relationship and the service levels that cause a relationship to break, giving you a new problem to fix.

How we can learn from the ancients

As anyone with a classical education will know, the answer to the budgeting process and its applications could be found carved in stone on a temple that has stood for well over 2,500 years.

The temple at Delphi had three sentences on its entry:

- Know thyself.
- Nothing in excess.
- Make a pledge and mischief is nigh.

All of these statements, attributed to some of the Seven Sages of Ancient Greece, are useful to apply to business in our quest to try and do the optimal things always:

- Know who you are. Are you a rigid organisation, beholden to tradition, or does your company allow for flexibility of approach and thinking in its budget procedures? Use the budgeting process to fuel culture. Are your processes appropriate for both the culture you have and the culture you want to fuel?
- The budget process should be neither too strict nor too lenient. It's never going to be perfect anyway, so settle for finding the right balance.

- A budget can be seen as a pledge of the whole organisation, something for everyone to commit to, limiting unwelcome, extreme or erratic behaviours.

So as the one of us with Hellenic stepchildren has learned is usually for the best, let's let the Greeks have the final word.

- Build flexible, future-ready budgets that reflect reality, not ritual.
- Let common sense override outdated rigidity.
- And above all, reward the people who stick their neck out to defy expectations.

4.7 Always plan to review the plan

Many organisations become trapped by plans they made when circumstances were different. Treat plans as living documents, not declarations carved in stone. Schedule regular checks to ask whether strategy still makes sense. Above all, normalise the idea that changing a plan is often the bravest, most rational choice.

Death by GPS

We've all seen movies where the hero is lost and thirsty in the desert. Images of scorpions, the skulls and bones of long-departed animals, vultures perched on the ribcage, waiting. Nothing but the hot, relentless sun. It is usually the hero we find in this situation and it's the villain that's left them there. They are often filmed in one of the hottest places on earth: Death Valley in the US. We can't recall the last movie where the blame lay with GPS.

However, in real life nowadays, most of the people lost and killed in the desert are there because of what the rangers in Death Valley call 'death by GPS'. *Build for Visibility* is about more than data – it's about reflecting on whether the road you are on still leads to the destination you want. Even the best systems and processes warrant review, because otherwise as things change, guidance becomes guesswork.

One morning in March 2011, Albert and Rita Chretien left their home in British Colombia to drive to a trade show in Las Vegas. Deciding to take the scenic route, they took Idaho State Highway 51, figuring they would be able to pick up a turnoff and then use GPS to pick up US Route 93 all the way to Vegas. After getting lost and stuck, Rita stayed with the van and survived for 48 days eating nuts and berries before being found by rescuers. Albert had tried to search for help on foot. His body was found 18 months later.

There are plenty more tales, thankfully most far less serious than that, of people using vehicles in national parks, then being too trusting in the technology and allowing GPS to lead them astray, into the middle of nowhere, over a bridge that doesn't exist, into a lake, or off a cliff maybe. A sign perhaps, of modern times. But just occasionally, companies can also mess it up so bad that it becomes terminal.

In all the cases, we see people who followed a plan, with step-by-step instructions, to reach the destination they wanted. And they are obvious examples that sticking to the plan makes sense most of the time, except when it doesn't. Sometimes, you *can* deviate from the path that has been set out for you. There should still be a plan set out to reach your destination, but you must allow for flexibility.

In business, ignoring new data, market shifts or feedback makes course correction more expensive, so *Control the Cost of Change* by making sure your plans can bend before they break. In companies and nation states, these plans are our budgets. Sticking to it exactly makes sense most of the time. However, the modern world is highly unpredictable, so following budgets drawn up months earlier can be the equivalent of deciding to drive your car off a cliff.

Governmental budgets around the world are subject to scrutiny, and much debate and discussion during a new government's first few months in office: thousands of hours of planning, meeting and debating for something which, at best, is a guiding plan for the next 12 months, based on assumptions that will largely be irrelevant a quarter of the way in.

In companies, months are spent creating the budget and more time is taken up in meetings with management explaining the differences between that budget and whatever is the new reality. It all begs the question, are you creating a plan that you can then manage? Or are you managing to a plan that may no longer be optimal? Review regularly and keep *Spend with Purpose* in mind.

Smart spenders *expect* the plan to change, and plan accordingly. *Controlling the Cost of Change* means remembering that change doesn't often come for free, but resisting planning for it will make it more expensive in the long run.

Why this dependence on budgets?

We believe the main reason is that we humans have a huge need for a level of predictability, and the budget gives us some comfort, by enshrining some idea of the future in a document. Perhaps another reason is that we do not have too many reliable alternatives. Most people certainly feel that having a budget is better than not having a budget. Not having anything at all would feel too much like driving around in that desert without a destination, or GPS.

So, what's the smarter alternative? That depends on how much flexibility you can build in and how much control you are willing to let go.

- **Option 1. Empowered autonomy:** Set goals, give each unit a provisional budget and let them decide how to deploy it.
- **Option 2. Conditional budgets:** Use an 'if this, then that' model to build a decision tree. Tie spending levels to performance or milestones.
- **Option 3. Rolling reviews:** Treat the budget as a living document, formally revisiting on a bi-monthly or quarterly basis. You can build in degrees, releasing corresponding amounts of budget at 60/80/100/120% of last year, for example.

In any of these cases, it will be important to review whether the path we follow leads us to the desired destination or to the precipice. Just like if the man chose to carry the raft everywhere, if you cling to inherited plans you can end up being more uncomfortable than you planned for.

If, hypothetically, we have budgeted to open four more stores this year, but the results of the existing ones are not good, perhaps focusing efforts on improving these stores and not on opening more is more important than meeting the budget for the long-term health of the business, staff and customers.

Of course, here you're also considering whether *Enough is a Strategy*. Sustainability is an issue and, while wider society should tackle questions like 'Should we still expect to import fresh fruit all year round?', you can think about whether you *want* the growth we're conditioned to chase if, for example, it relies on creating a huge carbon footprint.

Recently when Pedro was out driving towards a client, the GPS gave him clear instructions to follow a road that went directly into a reservoir. Given it was obvious, he chose to turn back, but the instructions persisted in showing the same path. As a regular GPS user, he tends to follow it most of the time, but that doesn't mean he is not also paying attention to the road, a strategy that will always be correct, even when the GPS is not.

Likewise, there are some strategies that are always right, regardless of what happens in the world. Paying attention to cost containment and fostering a culture that perpetuates it is one of them.

chapter 5

Myths cost money

5.1 Do highest volumes mean the best conditions?

Many believe that more volume automatically means better pricing or value. But bigger deals often come with hidden costs. Weigh up whether volume really drives value in each context rather than assuming bigger is always better.

It is easy to assume that large volumes equal low prices. Supermarket logic: a twelve pack of loo roll is cheaper per roll than a four pack. From there, it is easy enough to get into a realm of thinking that higher volumes = lower prices.

Once you are talking about more complex B2B sales, it seems reasonable to assume that when enticed by the possibility of a large order, most salespeople will do their utmost to get it. It is certainly true that larger volumes can help to get better prices, but there is by no means a guarantee that this is the case. We have seen many small companies get better prices than their larger competitors, through superior market knowledge, better supplier matching, more impressive negotiation skills, or just plain good luck with timing.

The moment we approach the market can make a huge difference. *Seeing the Whole System* means understanding the suppliers' perspective and context – knowing their hunger and capacity can change your thinking. If the supplier's factory is operating at full capacity, serving large orders on top of that may only interest them if their margin for that order is substantial. Otherwise, it can seem like more effort than it is worth. If, on the other hand, the factory is hungry for production, a supplier might well sacrifice margin just to dilute fixed costs.

Knowing the level of 'hunger' from each supplier is essential to time the moment to approach them. We have seen this hunger / plenty phenomenon affect all the suppliers of a given industry at the same time and we've seen it affect some more than others. It can be seasonal or can go along with a more general crisis.

If all the suppliers you approach are hungry for production, you may get really good prices, but if production is at full capacity, you probably won't. If some are hungry and others are not (the most common scenario), then choosing which suppliers to approach will make all the difference. For some suppliers, large orders may be actively undesirable, as they would demand a great tie-in of capital for raw-materials, warehousing, stocks, etc. that they just cannot afford. You must get the balance right.

For example, you may know of a B2B courier brand and be predisposed to use them. However, if they are a huge multinational with thousands of enormous clients, and you are a relative cottage industry, you may not end up with the service levels you expect. Better instead perhaps, to find a smaller supplier you may not have heard of, with excellent customer service, for whom you are an important client.

Recently we saw this exact situation with two of our clients' logistics operations. These clients happen to compete in the same industry. Before our intervention, the smaller client was being served by a very large supplier, and the larger client had a relatively small logistics provider. In both cases, we've managed to help them to lower costs and improved their service by changing providers. The smaller client migrated their logistics operation to an average-sized supplier, eager to earn the business and provide good service, whereas the larger client migrated theirs to the largest provider – the same one that was performing poorly for the other client.

Because the fit is way better, these more suitable relationships now work. The supplier business is not a poor provider, but the client and supplier were wrong for each other. As we all know, when you are wrong for each other, it is better to move on. Market and product knowledge have a huge impact on the conditions you can get, independent of volume. Putting *Value before Cost* means we can spend smarter.

The salesperson is incentivised to get the best conditions possible for their company, so it is their job to take advantage of any knowledge gaps that the buyer may have. Since it is rare that they find buyers as knowledgeable as they are, this happens relatively often. The smaller you can make that knowledge gap, the better your conditions will be.

A reliable client with good planning for smaller orders may get better pricing than a customer who places larger orders but does so in a way that is haphazard and inconsistent. Some suppliers may apparently offer best conditions for large quantities but then compensate their margins by having hidden costs, like higher shipping costs, after-sales service costs or (as we will see later) damaging auto-renewals.

Finally, complacency often plays a part. Precisely because we are a large buyer, we *believe* we are getting the best conditions. Over time this may prevent us from discovering better opportunities with alternative suppliers. Your high volume is not necessarily a virtue. It's only good value if it drives strategic goals.

Even though in many cases higher volumes will lead to better conditions, there are quite a few reasons why it might not be the case. At least some of these tend to be present, adding to the probability that this myth may not hold up to scrutiny. As with the space pen, it is not about how much you spend; it's whether the money moves the mission forward. *Spend with Purpose*, and whether you are spending a lot or a little, don't assume volume is virtue.

5.2 Does global pricing beat local?

Globally negotiated pricing often fails to account for local market dynamics, relationships, or service requirements. While these frameworks may have their place, you must evaluate when local flexibility delivers more value.

Two friends are walking in the African savanna and decide to sit down and rest for a few minutes. They take off their shoes and relax. Suddenly, they see a lion is coming their way, fast. One of them stands and starts to run, barefoot. Realising his friend is still seated, putting on his shoes, the runner shouts back:

'Are you crazy? Do you think you can outrun a lion because you have your shoes on?' Whilst finishing tying his shoes, the other guy replies: 'I don't need to outrun the lion. I just need to outrun you.'

We first heard this story from one of our clients, the national CEO for a large corporation, with factories all over the world. His point was that his most important competitors were not other companies, but other factories from within the same corporation. Whenever the global headquarters won a client or project, it decided where to allocate its production.

The winner was the most competitive factory / country – the one able to run faster than its competitors. The factory that won each of these races got more sales, people and other resources. Inversely, if a country unit lost enough races, the factory was eventually shut down, the workers let go and the corporation would leave for greener pastures.

This CEO understood that to keep his business unit going, his team was constantly running to win. They had to keep the production up and the costs down. He was somewhat frustrated because he did not control many of his costs – headquarters did. He thought this hampered his ability to outrun his competitors / colleagues.

Was he right?

Most multinational companies negotiate many costs centrally and have global agreements, ranging from raw materials or packaging to insurance or even to the fruit served mid-morning. A smaller number give their local units total freedom to fully decide on their costs.

We can evaluate each approach on its merits. The global strategy is to negotiate every single cost centrally, down to the coffee brand in the vending machines. The main strengths are:

1 global agreements add huge volumes; they can allow you to get great pricing from global suppliers;
2 standardisation of specifications and products allows no room for local spend to deviate from norms; no maverick spending means clarity and control;
3 easier to interchange personnel, as they will encounter pretty much the same structure and suppliers wherever they move

The strengths of the local approach correspond with the weaknesses of the global. They are:

1 ability to profit from local suppliers' closer and better service levels;
2 suppliers can be easily adaptable to local standards and available products;
3 personnel are far more attuned to local suppliers and more motivated by being given the power to decide.

Which is the best approach? The good news is we can reply with only two words; the bad news is the two words are 'it depends'. It depends on what the company does. It depends on what the company needs to buy and at what level of quality.

It depends whereabouts in the world its offices, factories or depots are located. It depends also on the company culture and many other things.

Both strategies have their strengths and weaknesses. Relying on any one of them involves compromise. There is little logic to global vs local, so there is no place for assumptions. Focus on what fits your timelines, your systems and objectives.

Even McDonalds, the epitome of standardisation, adapts many parts of its marketing mix. Although there are standards you can expect to be almost identical everywhere in the world, McDonald's holds firmly to most procedures, the dimension of the buns, the burgers you can expect anywhere you go and how long it takes to cook the fries.

However, they do adapt some things.

- **Product** – serves beer in many countries, sausages in Germany, has Halal certification in Muslim countries, replaces beef for chicken and mutton in India, serves shrimp burgers and green tea ice-cream in Japan.
- **Place** – in places like Madrid it sits in a palace, in Oporto in an Art Deco building, in Bergen the McDonald's is a typical wooden hut and there is even one on a decommissioned airplane in Taupo, New Zealand.
- **Price** – different prices defined for each country even within the Eurozone, for example.
- **Promotion** – in China, Ronald McDonald has a female companion, Aunt McDonald. In East Asia communication is much more geared to the new generations.

So, how do you find the best path? Three-thousand-year-old Greek mythology provides the answer. The modern interpretation of the tale of Icarus tends to stand as a warning of the dangers of unchecked ambition – don't fly too close to the sun as a euphemism for stay humble. But did you know that Icarus' father warned him not to fly too low across the sea, so as not to dampen the carefully crafted wings, as well as not to fly too high?

It's like the Goldilocks principle. Not too hot, not too cold. It all coincides with our own experience: the best path between local or global lies somewhere in the middle. In some cost areas, there may be a huge advantage in prices being negotiated by global headquarters. Some raw materials or parts may enjoy volume discounts. And a lot happens in the clouds. Having the same card gateway, networking provider or software licenses may not only guarantee a better price but also better support.

Owning one factory, you insure against fire. Own ten and a single group policy, capped at two total losses, gives you the protection you need at a much better rate. If you suffer three losses in a year, either the world's ending, or you've made some dangerous enemies.

The insurer would be able to set a way better price than if he had to cover all ten on its own. So, does this make insurance a good category to be managed centrally? For most of it, the answer will be 'yes', but there are usually some types of risk better covered at a national level, either because each country has its own regulations or because some deviation or flexibility is necessary. Vehicle, worker compensation and health insurance usually fall more into the local camp.

Only by *Seeing the Whole System* – tax, regulation, usage, risk and employee feedback – can you make the right call. In complex areas like this, surface level logic will not be enough.

Going into other categories, your fleet costs may enjoy discounts negotiated with carmakers for a region (Europe, North America, etc.), but the definition of the models will probably work best handled at a national level, as the fiscal penalties or incentives around both employer and employee tax statuses vary wildly between countries. Even for the same job, an electric vehicle may be the best solution in a certain country, but diesel may still present the best overall total cost of ownership across the border.

International logistics are another area that can sometimes benefit from central negotiations, but onward national distribution is best dealt with in each country. Air travel may profit from central organisation, although it may come at the cost of losing some flexibility. Most other costs will probably be handled best at a national level. The proximity to the suppliers, their offers and capabilities, as well as a better fit between the needs and the available market solutions, will most often translate into better service and costs for the purchaser.

What about organisations with multiple locations within the same country? That picture can be a little clearer, since for most organisations it is best to handle all costs at a central point. Having one person or team responsible for each category is usually far better than having each local office or shop do it themselves.

There are exceptions. In larger countries and companies, it may make sense to divide the responsibility over some costs into regions. Another exception are factories. They usually have local needs for areas like parts or maintenance, which are best handled at that level.

So, what, if anything, you can do about it? Finding someone to deal with some costs centrally may be relatively easier, as it may find its way to someone searching for ways to expand their powers. Going in the other direction can be more difficult, for the very same reason. As the writer Upton Sinclair puts it, *'It is difficult to get someone to understand something, when their salary depends on not understanding it.'*

In our previous professional lives, working for multinationals, we have found one method that often works: searching for better solutions and prices with local suppliers and then presenting them to someone in headquarters who can win from the savings, but not lose their power with that change. As companies grow, complexity multiplies. Don't choose global or local by default. Design with intention. A balanced strategy doesn't come from adhering to a policy.

5.3 'We got three quotes' (What can possibly go wrong?)

Comparing prices from three suppliers guarantees neither competition nor quality, yet if we had a dollar for every time we've heard it, we'd retire. Flawed specifications or a shallow understanding of needs can also undermine a tokenistic process.

For a range of cultural reasons, the number three resonates. Liberté, égalité, fraternité. Life, liberty and the pursuit of freedom. Blood, sweat and tears. The father, the son and the holy spirit. Reduce, reuse, recycle. According to psychology, this 'triadic' structure allows us to remember more tightly than pairs or quartets.

Imagine an executive who attributed his success to believing there is a magic number. He believed in the power of this number to the extent that he believed it could resolve any situation in his favour. If he had to solve a problem, he thought of three solutions. Planning the future, he considered three scenarios. Speaking on any subject, he summarised everything into three topics.

One day he was lost in a strange city and asked a stranger for directions how to get to his destination. For him, the answer made perfect sense. 'Go straight ahead, take the third left three times and walk straight for another 500 metres.' He scrupulously followed the directions… and walked around in a circle ending up right back where he started.

Strange as it may seem, in many companies this obsession with the number three is very much alive. One of their signs is that when asked about their purchasing policy, many think they are following best practice by consulting three suppliers and choosing the cheapest.

If you are looking in a supplier pool of 100 potential companies, the odds of getting the best three for your requirements by chance are slim. If you *Spend with Purpose* this is supposed to be aligned with your core mission, not just a box-ticking exercise. The responsibility is to actively manage the situation, not blindly follow a checklist. Even if you do identify the best three suppliers for you, what if one of them is almost always the same big player in the sector, and everyone else identifies them similarly?

It's possible that your process becomes a farce because the other two are so used to losing against their competitor that they put little effort into it and respond out of courtesy, but with little real effort to capture the business. If you don't use some sort of criteria, you might still pick three from the upper 20% of pricing and conclude there is little to choose between them, when you've missed 80% of the market.

This is particularly true in some areas of overhead cost management, where focus fades. Suppliers are more likely to invest in increasing margin over the course of a contract, especially in these overlooked areas, since they know you are unlikely to be following it closely. Being able to generate the best conditions can mean creating effective competition between suppliers of the same products or services.

Even if we accept that the company was able to choose the best three suppliers in the entire market *for them*, and that they encourage real competition between them, the conditions still may not be the best. Cost isn't the only consideration. Take for example the humble brown box. By getting three good quotes for this box we can think we have the best solution. But there are a whole range of other details we could be questioning that could lead to much more profitable solutions.

Is it possible to use alternative materials? Can the thickness be reduced without losing quality upon delivery? Should the thickness be increased to reduce breakages? Are there other materials that can better package the merchandise? Is it possible to reuse it? Does everything need to go in the same kind of box? Think about millimetres. Can the primary packaging size be slightly reduced? Perhaps a similarly small change to the primary packaging can mean more items in a crate, more on a pallet, more in the container and compound the effect of savings on the shipping cost per item.

The best is the one that is the best *fit* between the company's qualitative needs and a wide range of other variables. The number of quotes is not the metric; the quality of thinking is.

In one country's central government departments, three quotes for office supplies came from three different suppliers but they were all sourced from the same wholesaler. Prices, specs, even stock codes were near-identical. There was the semblance of process, but they were in a hall of mirrors. Competitive pricing was an illusion. *Build for Visibility* isn't about how many vendors you see, but how clearly you are seeing. For the executive in the story, three may be the magic number sometimes, but choose it all the time, and you might just keep going round in circles.

5.4 Most expensive means best

> *Premium options can create a comforting illusion of quality but often fail to deliver commensurate value. Price should be tested against outcomes, not assumed to be a proxy for capability.*

Do you believe that paying more for something is likely to mean better quality? *Value before Cost* reminds us that it doesn't necessarily stand to reason. A high price is not evidence. Price plays a large part in your forming an opinion about a product or service, even if subconsciously. We are conditioned to one extent or another.

Take the experiment conducted by Dan Ariely, James B Duke Professor of psychology and behavioural economics at Duke University. If you were given the same medicine, do you think knowing its price would make the effects greater or lesser, depending on whether it was more expensive or cheaper? In the abstract, we will all agree that it shouldn't make any difference. A medicine should be as effective as the active ingredients: for the same medicine, the effects should be the same.

Interestingly, this is not what happens. In the study by Ariely and others, the people taking the same pill who were told that it cost $2.50 noticed more pain-reducing effects than the group told the pill cost 10 cents. Similar studies have been carried out relating to varying levels of spend from wine to electronics and cars. In all these cases, most people associated better quality with the more expensive products, even though in these examples too, the products were strictly the same.

These data indicate a myth that we all believe to a greater extent than we think: that something more expensive is necessarily better. It is true that in most cases, something more expensive is usually better than a similar, cheaper product. Sometimes a lot better, compounding our bias. Because our brains are very efficient at forming patterns, they take high frequency as an automatic rule, which we rarely question.

Price sits alongside other prevailing beliefs regarding shopping, meaning marketers have room to manipulate us, in at least two ways. The first involves setting a very high price for a product. An expensive price tag leads us to think of a product as luxurious and high in quality. The additional advantage of this strategy, in addition to increasing the margin of that product, is that this perception often extends to the rest of the brand's portfolio, meaning that even those products with a reasonable price benefit from this halo effect of greater perceived quality across the brand.

The second way used to leverage this effect is to set an *artificially* high price and then offer a large discount. The customer will tend to associate high quality with the supposed initial price, thinking they are getting a great deal. To find examples, just go to any supermarket where you will easily find many wines with 30% or even 50% discounts. This pricing as theatre is to be ignored, largely, unless it happens to connect back to *Purpose*.

We've all overpaid when we've been told a good story, and we'll probably let it happen again. We will all fail sometimes; there is always room for improvement. Being able to experiment without knowing how much it costs (blind wine tastings, for example) will help reduce this effect even further, even if those opportunities in business are harder to create.

In Ariely's drug study, 85% of the participants who tried the more expensive pill found that it reduced their pain. However, just like the cheaper one, it contained no active ingredient. They were both pure placebos and yet they worked. Our brains are governed by mysterious logic. Far better to recognise it and plan accordingly than to pretend you are immune. Investigate thoroughly, gain knowledge enthusiastically and ensure research and not assumption underpins your process.

5.5 Lowest cost must mean best value

Conversely, chasing the lowest price can also backfire. Initial savings can evaporate through increased maintenance, reduced service, or higher downstream costs. Weigh total value over the full lifecycle rather than fixating on upfront prices.

Deliberately choosing the cheapest option *can* be the best decision you can make, but it depends entirely on what you are buying and whether it makes sense in the context of clear objectives. Electricity comes down the same cables, from the same sources, so the logo on the top of the bill should not matter.

Right? Well, even in this case, no. There are other factors. The type of contract offered (fixed, indexed or hybrid), the length of the contract, the customer service of the supplier, their financial stability, the payment conditions.

When comparing a total commodity, the lowest price may be the deciding factor most of the time. But even with a commodity, the lowest price won't always be the deciding factor. The more you introduce a bit of additional complexity, the less true this myth becomes. If you are buying a heavy production machine, try to *See the Whole System* – recognise the lifecycle costs that a cheaper price tag can obscure. Considerations like reliability, quality or service, output capacity, as well as total cost of ownership (which may include service and parts prices, energy consumption, etc.) will have to be put well above price alone.

We are best served by the solution that provides the best value for our intended use. Price is an important variable, but it shouldn't be considered on its own. Just as the most expensive is not always the best, so the cheapest is not always the most appropriate. Often, these preoccupations with price, before value, are the decisions that lead to poor reliability, higher operating overheads and silent profit leaks. In our experience, evaluating any solution based on price alone would be a mistake in nearly all cases.

5.6 The superiority illusion (why believing you do this well is probably wrong)

Many people are confident they manage overheads well. Overconfidence creates blind spots and misses opportunities. Even competent organisations can benefit from external perspective and a willingness to re-examine the basics.

Studies show that 94% of university professors believe they are superior to their colleagues (Cross, 1977), 87% of MBA students rank themselves above their peers (*Stanford GSB Reporter*, 2000), 80% of drivers think they are better than average (Svenson, 1981) and 25% of students think they are in the top 1% for leadership skills (Alicke and Govorun, 2005). These numbers come from different studies, all carried out by reputable universities. Based on other studies, we can add plenty to the list of fields in which we tend to consider ourselves better than most others: health, happiness, memory, popularity, relationships, intelligence, stock trading, etc.

This phenomenon is called 'Illusory Superiority' and is prevalent in us humans (especially in westerners). It's defined as 'cognitive bias in which a person overestimates their own qualities and abilities, in relation to the same qualities and abilities of other people'. Interestingly, one of its effects is that we also believe that, unlike others, we are less susceptible to this and other biases. Illusory Superiority is also very limiting: if 94% of teachers think they are better than average, what is their incentive to learn and improve?

Unskilled and unaware

The concept of illusory superiority is also evident in what has become known as the Dunning Kruger effect. In the 1990s, two scientists at Cornell University conducted a study which attempted to discover whether incompetent people were aware of their incompetence. To do this, the researchers gave 45 undergraduate students a 20-question logic test and then asked them to rate their own performance in two different ways.

The first asked them to estimate how many of the questions they got correct; the second was to see how that compared with their fellow students who took the test. The lowest scoring students scored an average of 10/20 and the highest an average of 17/20. Both estimated they scored around 14, so their self-assessment was off, with the lowest scoring students overestimating their performance and the highest scoring underestimating theirs.

Their assessment of themselves against their peers was where the 'I'm the best' attitude was on full display. Those lower-scoring students still estimated that they did better than 62% of their fellow students, and the higher scoring ones thought they scored better than 68% of their peers. Some of them were correct, but the lowest scoring students overestimated their performance substantially.

Business attitudes to cost management

You can probably guess by now why we have brought this up. Although we don't have any university studies to support this, we do feel quite confident in saying that in relation to cost management in companies, this bias is ever present. Almost all managers, directors and business owners we deal with believe that their company is better than average at controlling costs, and that by and large, they have them well under control.

That's why it is so important to *Challenge Assumptions*, because it's not just personal bias, it creates operational risk. They won't all be right. It is far, far more likely that they are overestimating their abilities, *and* those of their colleagues. Paradoxically, the truth is that the more convinced we are of our own superiority, the worse off we are since that biased – and incorrect – assumption gives us less motivation to do better.

In our experience the greater the certainty a manager has that 'costs are under control', the more flags it should raise. They are probably carrying a false sense of security based on nothing but tradition and conformity.

To counter this bias, which we all have, the best thing to do would be to ask ourselves:

1. What are the cost areas in which I am most certain of my / our superiority?
2. Among these, which ones I am less sure about could be costing me the most?
3. If I accept that I am weaker in these areas than I thought, how can I improve?

Changing perceptions of ourselves and our organisation is difficult, as it challenges our self-image and risks upsetting the status quo. But it is important to do it. Partly because we need to challenge the 'way we've always done things' regularly anyway, but mostly because it can allow us to make a Kobayashi-style quantum leap with our results in these areas.

We live in challenging times and reflecting on these issues now can pay dividends; after all, it is well known that with any crisis comes opportunity. Those who are best prepared are the ones likely to take most advantage.

Try this:

What are the areas where you think you already do better than most and how would you know if you are right or wrong? Are you ready to look at this and question your assumptions in detail?

References

Alicke, M.D. and Govorun, O. (2005) 'The better-than-average effect'. In Alicke, M.D., Dunning, D.A. and Krueger, J.I. (eds) *The Self in Social Judgment. Studies in Self and Identity*. Psychology Press, pp. 85–106.

Cross, K.P. (Spring 1977) *Not Can But Will College Teachers Be Improved?*. New Directions for Higher Education.

Sinclair, U. (1935) *I Candidate for Governor: And how I got licked*. California University Press.

Stanford GSB Reporter (2000, 24 April) *'It's Academic.' 2000*, pp. 14–5. via Zuckerman, E.W. and Jost, J.T. (2001) What makes you think you're so popular? Self Evaluation maintenance and the subjective side of the 'friendship paradox'. *Social Psychology Quarterly*, 64 (3): 207–223.

Svenson, O. (February 1981) Are we all less risky and more skillful than our fellow drivers?'. *Acta Psychologica*.

chapter 6

Making change happen

6.1 Triggering a cost optimisation process

Most cost management projects start reactively. We should create internal triggers to drive improvement before trouble hits. Instead of waiting for urgency, create a sense of constructive discontent as the starting point for lasting transformation.

Businesses all exist for the same reason. Typically, they will provide a product or service to people and must attract and retain customers if they wish to grow. All businesses seek to make a profit to continue to exist. In fact, in famed 20th-century economist Milton Friedman's 'doctrine', he argued that no company has a responsibility to the public or society, and that its only responsibility is to its shareholders.

According to this logic, the responsibility of the board of any company is to maximise profits for the shareholders. As we will see later, some would now challenge that view, but it remains a dominant influence on corporate governance. Monies may be retained to reinvest in hiring more staff, or is allocated to innovation, research & development, but ultimately (long-term) shareholder returns take primacy when making decisions on behalf of the business.

One should therefore be surprised to find that companies do not routinely enough seek out ways to maximise shareholder returns by focusing on cost, instead getting stuck using the age-old modus operandi. *Profit Fuels Progress* should take control, realising that cost isn't an imposed mechanism that you must survive; it's strategy.

Organisations may decide to embark on a cost-reduction programme, in response to internal or external pressures. Without *Controlling the Cost of Change* though, even the best intentions stall. Diagnosing a reason to act is only half the problem; you also need a roadmap for the project, and adoption. Often, projects stem from the need to improve the financial health or operational efficiency of the business or come about as a need to adapt to changing external circumstances.

These are the main reasons why any organisation may need to prioritise cost-reduction:

- financial distress
- economic downturn
- industry changes
- mergers & acquisitions
- declining profit margins
- operational inefficiencies
- technological change
- global events
- strategic repositioning
- rising costs
- legislation
- shareholder pressure

While these triggers are diverse, their effects are not isolated. *See the Whole System* reminds us that changing cost dynamics in one area will echo elsewhere, sometimes where you least expect it. It is important to note that companies occasionally implement cost-saving measures as part of a broader strategy to enhance overall performance and competitiveness. The specific triggers can vary, but many of them are reactive or couched in negativity. Only *sometimes* do companies implement these measures as part of a broader strategy. All too frequently, they are a reaction to some sort of threat. Yet shouldn't we fix the roof while the sun's out?

We already know that implementing these strategies when the business is buoyant will have more effect. Instead of mitigating losses, reacting to circumstance or trying to navigate a storm, creating extra value in good times can help with cashflow, investment and growth.

There are also plenty of reasons *not* to embark on a cost-management programme. While cost optimisation programmes can bring about various benefits, there are also challenges and reasons why companies may hesitate or face difficulties in engaging with such initiatives. For balance, here are some reasons why companies may NOT want to embark on a cost optimisation programme:

- short-term focus
- fear of impact on morale
- lack of leadership support
- resistance to change
- perceived quality impact
- overemphasis on growth
- investment in growth
- lack of visibility into costs
- perceived complexity of implementation
- sunk cost fallacy
- lack of benchmarking data
- market volatility
- dependency on suppliers
- regulatory constraints
- prioritisation of innovation

It's essential for companies to carefully weigh the pros and cons, considering their unique circumstances, strategic goals and the potential impact on stakeholders when deciding whether to engage in cost optimisation programmes.

But look closely and most of these reasons fall apart. They are excuses, not strategy. If they are the only things standing between you and a more efficient, more profitable business, walk past them.

The best excuse – the only genuinely valid reason – is lacking the specific knowledge and expertise to do any better. We've already demonstrated how you can find the time. Any organisation that is comfortable with the results achieved has little motivation for change. A cost reduction process will always imply some change beyond the simple price, whether of suppliers, products or processes. But change is constant, change can also be for the better, and change need not be feared.

Companies can behave like hamsters that jump between the two wheels in their cages. For a few years they run without stopping on the sales wheel. When the external factors hit, they react. Everything jumps to the cost wheel, until the pressure reduces and everyone jumps back to the first wheel. In efficient, successful and forward-thinking organisations, there is an ever-present culture of looking at both sides of the results statement, making cost optimisation a constant: a clear understanding that it is impossible for all knowledge to reside within the company, that looking for external inputs can enrich the corporate culture of continuous improvement.

These days, we might argue that Milton Freidman's argument is starting to show its age. Throughout the latter half of the 20th century and especially in the 21st, humanity has increasingly understood that we are living on an earth made up of finite resources. What we now tend to call 'sustainability' – though that has many definitions which we'll get to later – has meant organisations are increasingly forced to think more about their social and public responsibilities in a way that they did not foresee.

Carrying out a process like this is about not waiting for a problem. It's about using cost strategy as a tool for resilience, performance and growth – before you are forced to.

6.2 Learning what you can and cannot control

Focus energy where it can make a difference. Stop wasting time railing against markets or regulation and instead double down on internal improvements.

'God, grant me the serenity to accept the things I cannot change, the courage to change the things I can, and the wisdom to know the difference.'

Most of us will recognise the serenity prayer. It was created by theologian Reinhold Niebuhr in the 1930s and swiftly – and famously – adopted by Alcoholics Anonymous. We are not here to chastise your refreshment habits. We are here to remind you to focus your limited time only on what is important. It's the essence of *Spend with Purpose*.

Most organisations run lean. Some sectors and businesses enjoy substantial profit margins, but most businesses in retail and manufacturing will run a single percentage profit margin. This tends to mean that they are heavily focused on their purchasing in key areas. For a retailer, that is on goods for resale. For example, a supermarket chain will have buyers for meat, wine, cheese etc. and a department store for clothing, homeware and electronics. It is their responsibility to source the required quality of appropriate goods and produce, befitting their brand, with the required reliability of delivery, and at a cost that enables them to sell at a price that will generate profit in their market.

A large manufacturer in the automotive supply-chain will similarly have procurement teams dedicated to purchasing raw materials and parts of the requisite quality at the right price, to design and build high-quality products. These businesses well understand the value of having in place experts to manage the supply market, run tender processes, collaborate and innovate with suppliers, and deliver increasing value. In their core business, they manage these costs every day.

Of course, you cannot control everything. And controlling the cost is only part of the story. Sales and money in are the driving force of any company. Without paying clients, there is no business at all. Businesses like Nestlé and Coca-Cola, with famous brands, unique products and sales in multiple global markets have greater consistency and predictability of revenue and profit margins, because they have devolved risk and the power to manage costs effectively with smaller suppliers. They are still, to some extent, at the same risk of market volatility in some areas, they just have more room to spread those costs around.

Commodities bought on markets such as the London Metals Exchange are subject to market forces and beyond the control of most organisations, but as we will see, there are still steps you can take. You may not be able to control the wars in the Middle East and the subsequent increase in the energy price, but you can do more about it than just accepting the renewal price when it comes along. You can prepare in advance, you can look at other suppliers, you can change what you buy, you can change how you buy it, you can reduce what you use, you can invest in renewable energy.

We discussed the vital importance of sales. But what if paying clients suddenly disappear? We all learned many things during the COVID pandemic, but when your business is forced by law to close and sales fall to zero, there are not too many options on the table. It is not just the businesses forced into closure that suffered. Overnight, their suppliers had nobody to sell to either. Entrepreneurs and business owners saw the last holy cow that they could rely on and influence – at least to some extent – drop dead.

Basically, their options were:

1. reinvent or pivot to online (like restaurants pivoting to home delivery), or pivot to new markets (like garment manufacturers pivoting to facemasks);
2. focus on cutting costs.

Necessity is often the mother of invention. Until COVID came along and shook things up nobody thought they had to really think like that at all. Now businesses should be more concerned about what happens next time. Some businesses thrived during the pandemic – streaming services, takeaway apps, delivery services, toilet paper manufacturers and healthcare companies making hand sanitiser and PPE saw sales soaring to unprecedented levels.

But what if you are not one of the businesses that benefitted from the circumstances surrounding COVID? What if you are not Coca-Cola, or BMW, who can spread the risk, but a much smaller business? What should you focus on and how can you more effectively manage your own business costs to maximise your own profits. After all, you work hard for them, so why should some of it be sitting in the bank accounts of your suppliers?

To add more value to businesses like those – businesses like yours – to squeeze out a few more percentage points of profit requires deeper thought and a bolder approach. The other thing it requires is an appetite for a little change. Because the odds are against you having the advantages of those international behemoths, your control of costs tends to be less than full.

With our experience, we can convincingly argue that the influence we can have on the cost side of the business is greater than the sales team can achieve on the sales side. That might sound like a bold statement, but beyond an anomalous surge driving down costs is a far easier process than driving up sales. It also makes more sense. We believe it's a lot easier to find 20% savings in overheads than it is to grow your business 20%. In fact, we know it is.

Let us once more take metals as an example: if your inputs depend on steel, the variations of the London Metal Exchange will mean increases or decreases in your purchasing price. Even so, there are a variety of strategies you could follow to exert some control over the prices. You could:

- improve the spread you are paying over the index
- search for new suppliers that can provide better conditions
- centre and commit purchases to one supplier only, who offers better conditions
- enter into long-term agreements with fixed prices
- use financial derivatives to fix prices either wholly or partly
- reduce usage / waste / stock.

These are just some examples of where you can be wiser in terms of what to focus on and what will bring rewards. Of course, nobody has the time to get to everything. But using Pareto's 80/20 rule and ignoring most of the overhead costs that fall into the 20% is the equivalent of knocking off 90 minutes early every day. Use the rule to accept that there are some areas that are not worth controlling (perhaps 20% of the 20%) but use all the time you can find to do something about the rest.

Accept that there are different ways to approach the problems at different levels. Your core team looks after your core business. You pay them well, but you do not need an £100k/year managed print expert employed 100% of the time. But if you spend hundreds of thousands, even millions of euros on a managed print contract over the course of a 5-year contract length, it might be worth having one on hand during negotiations.

There are other things you can control during aspects of the costing, purchasing and usage process. A few with impact on your company's results are:

- **processes** – reducing the time it takes to do some tasks, the stocks or waste, will have a strong impact
- **human resources** – hiring, motivation and tasks assigned
- **purchasing** – centralised or decentralised, frequency of other rules
- **suppliers** – having too many or too few suppliers for each cost category, suppliers that are not a perfect fit for your needs, too long or too short agreements, geographically close or far
- **fixed vs variable costs** – for instance, you can choose to subcontract services
- **communication channels** – both inside and outside the organisation.

We will explore these factors throughout this book. For now, be aware they impact your results and are actionable. As the serenity prayer puts it, the wisdom to distinguish between what we can and cannot control may be the most important part of running our lives, as well as our businesses.

6.3 Never ask a barber if you need a haircut

Suppliers can recommend solutions that serve their own interests. Outsourcing judgment to them creates hidden costs and poor outcomes. Independent thinking and critical challenge are essential to protect value.

There is a story, relayed by Yuval Noah Harari in *Homo Deus* (2017), that during the late 1980s Mikhail Gorbachev sent a close Soviet aide to London. For a long time after the Second World War, a theory pervaded that the Soviet Union's communist and socialist economy would eventually overtake the United States. In the event, the Soviet Union broke up before this ever happened. Despite the initial optimism, there were many ways in which life for the people of the communist USSR was tough.

It was with this in mind that Gorbachev sent his aide to England. He wanted to learn about what the British were doing well, and the aide was given a warm welcome and taken around London to both the LSEs (The London School of Economics *and* the London Stock Exchange). During the tour, the Soviet aide became interested in the contrasts he observed with home. You may remember something of the queues for bread in the USSR. Like everything else, bread distribution in Moscow and beyond was managed by the state, yet there were always long queues and shortages throughout the empire.

In London, the official could not help but notice that despite being in a city of millions, he had not seen a single line outside a bakery or grocery store. The bread distribution system seemed to provide abundance in multiple points of sale, expeditious supply, an absence of queues, and reasonable prices. He asked to meet the person responsible for bread distribution in the city.

Of course there *was* no central planning in London. The government left it for the market to provide. No single person, or even a single entity could coordinate the supply of bread to a large city as well as the market does. The individual decisions of each entrepreneur combined to make everything work. Competition ensures that waste is controlled, and prices are reasonable.

Still, it would be naive to think that any markets are completely efficient. One of the professions that contributes most to the modern market's efficiency is sales. By communicating their product knowledge, they become sources of information about their sector. This allows smarter buyers to become familiar with the options that exist.

Unfortunately, sales professionals also contribute to the *inefficiency* of markets. That same motivation to sell *their* offering makes them keen to differentiate from their competitors. Different information can make comparison difficult for buyers.

You may recall that at the Berkshire Hathaway AGM in 1994, Warren Buffet cautioned delegates: *'never ask a barber if you need a haircut'.*

The barber is an interested party; how he responds might be motivated by his own self-interest, rather than what is best for you. This can happen in any B2B client / supplier relationship. Good salespeople will find good reasons for you to buy more of their product or service. An account manager's job is to grow the account.

Recognising you will never know the supplier's sector as well as they do themselves is why *Build for Visibility* matters. There are multiple influences, opportunities and threats to the product or service that only insiders can know. You might not know as much as your supplier does about their sector, but tender experience, involving knowledgeable stakeholders and reviewing previous performance data, all close the gap.

To get closest to having a good understanding of the market and what is available, you can run a tender process and ask the appropriate entities to pitch for the business. Each of them will have their own agendas and objectives. They will analyse the information cautiously, with a dose of rational scepticism. After all, they only have a *one in x* chance of winning anyway.

To the information they collect from suppliers, buyers should add other sources. They can use colleagues from other companies, friends, external consultants, or online research. Whatever you can learn, don't get complacent – remember you are still an outsider. Confidence built on assumptions is more dangerous than acknowledged ignorance. Remember to not carry forward what once served you but no longer applies.

Complacency can be harmful in a negotiation. Humility is more advantageous. Information asymmetry will always exist, reducing it and mitigating its effect is usually the best you can achieve. That's why *Seeing the Whole System* is so vital. Good buyers are not just gatekeepers of cost, they provide perspective. Don't think you need to know everything, just connect enough dots to minimise risk and be discerning.

6.4 What we don't see can eat profit

Hidden costs and quiet inefficiencies slowly corrode margin: unmonitored contracts, automatic renewals and untested assumptions compound. Develop routines for surfacing the unseen and confront what everyone assumes is fine.

Dutchman Antonie van Leeuwenhoek is commonly acknowledged as the father of modern microbiology. His 1677 paper, 'Concerning little animals' gives the first account of bacteria, living in different environments. Jospeh Lister (born 1827), a British surgeon, was the first to apply so-called 'germ theory' to surgery, helping to cement the understanding of 'antiseptic medicine'. They proved that things invisible to the naked eye can be fatal.

A friend once told us he was very confused when he spoke to his accountant. Despite the profits that our friend's company was making, he seemed to have cash flow difficulties every month. 'How is it possible?' he asked. 'Every month I make profits and every month it is difficult to find the money to pay my staff, our suppliers, and our taxes? Shouldn't there be some money left over?!'

This friend, like many other businesspeople, had difficulty separating his profit from his cashflow. Profit is the theoretical leftover. It is useful for calculating taxes and showing to the banks, but it is cashflow that allows you to pay everyone who provides services to the company and remunerate shareholders. That money is the lifeblood of the company. It's exactly why *Build for Visibility* matters. If you can't see the cashflow reality – the movement of money, not just the appearance of it – then strategic decision-making becomes guesswork.

Even a profitable business can be cash-strapped if visibility is lacking. So, what is it exactly that separates the profit from the cashflow? On the input side, the moment the invoice is issued, it is there in the accounts and thus considered when calculating profits. However, only when the invoice is paid does the money come in. The greater this time lag, the greater the discrepancy between the ideas of profit and cashflow.

In an extreme case, where a customer takes several months to pay, you may even have to pay your VAT bill to the state, without having received the monies from the customer. For example, for a sale of £1,000, you advance your 20% to the state. Profit currently looks like £800, but your cashflow is £200 down.

On the outgoings side, something similar happens with receipts, but here in the opposite way. This time, the longer the payment deadlines, the greater the difference between the two concepts, but this time in your favour.

There are also three other factors: stock, investments and financing. If we acquire stocks that are idle, then accounting is neutral, but the money has gone out of the bank. Whenever we acquire new equipment or machinery, in accounting terms the cost is spread over several years, but the money may all come out now, or in instalments. Instalments seldom match the amortisation timeline.

Financing, from banks or other partners, can have a positive sign in cash flow (money coming in) or negative. We suggested to our friend that they ask their accountant for some additional line items to be added to the reports that had confused them so much. These were:

1. stock variation
2. investments (excluding amortisations)
3. variation in debtors
4. variation of creditors (including banks, partners, etc.)

This gave our friend a much more detailed picture of how much money they were earning or losing each month. Visibility is key. Actionable data makes for better decision-making. Most companies don't suffer with poor numbers; they suffer from a lack of numbers or ones that are poorly framed.

Where we work in the field of cost optimisation, the relationship is normally simple and direct: a pound that is not spent is worth the same as a pound in profit and a pound cash in the treasury. It is therefore an excellent area to work on to improve any organisations financial results, because they will be tangible and visible, wherever they are. Many companies fail, not because they are not 'making profit', but because they lack the liquidity to pay staff and suppliers and continue to trade.

We learned an awful lot about ourselves during the pandemic, but surely one of the greatest lessons of 2020 was to take a much closer look at liquidity. After all, in finance – as in medicine – it is what we cannot see that kills us.

6.5 High-wire artists wanted – you must be brave

Cost transformation is a test of courage. Challenging sacred cows and questioning old habits can feel risky, but the right balance is necessary for real progress. See discomfort as proof you are doing the hard work that matters.

In 1974 'Man on Wire' Philippe Petit crossed the 42 metres (138 feet) between New York's Twin Towers, balancing on a steel cable. At 410 metres of altitude (1,345 feet) he walked, danced, laid down and waved at the crowd, way below. It was a unique demonstration of art and will.

Great feats like this do not happen without preparation. Petit planned this stunt for 6 years. Training his mind and body for the physical demands was only part of the task. He had to find how to illegally enter the towers, get to the top and install the wire during the night, before sunrise. He had to anticipate the effects of the climate and wind on his performance. This is exactly what *Control the Cost of Change* is reminding us to price in.

The real cost isn't just the moment of action, it's the scaffolding beneath it all: the training, integration and the preparation that rarely appears in budget lines. In business, the balance between threats and opportunities mean each of us is a Philippe Petit. We must prepare the company for the challenges ahead, and at each step, stop, check the wind speed and direction before advancing.

The line is narrow, the fall deadly. Unlike on the high wire, where a mistake has immediate consequence, the effect of a business decision can take years to unfold. Do we invest more in advertising, or cut back? Do we risk capital, or protect the reserves?

During a pandemic, decisions about health and safety become as important as they were for the high-wire artist. At the extremes lie two unsustainable scenarios: either fully stop all operations or continue as if nothing is happening. In the middle, a thousand options. It's a good reminder to *Challenge*

Assumptions. Extremes are easier to define, but smarter spending encourages us to realise that there is no need for binary thinking. Just ask better questions so you know where you stand. As if a health crisis was not enough, governments also erected hurdles. Keeping up with the constant changes in rules, laws or subsidies required the skills of a contortionist.

Besides the planning in resilience, Petit's feat had other aspects we can learn from. Before stepping solo on the wire, he took every opportunity to recruit allies to his cause, whether to help him circumvent security of the building, to help secure the cable or take photos. He had to motivate those team members with a shared ambitious vision. He was open to new ideas, either from his team or outside it, integrating the best ones.

Every element of his approach translates into a business context. This is what '*Spend to Strengthen*' asks of us: to invest in cohesion, alignment and shared confidence. The tightrope isn't just walked across. It's held in place by people who believe.

All kinds of forces can push our companies from the high wire. Keeping your balance isn't just a metaphor. In a business context it means the difference between cash-positive resilience and a slow-motion fall.

6.6 If your options are limited, invent the wheel

Many constraints are self-imposed. Challenge whether limits on budget, process, or ambition are truly fixed or just inherited assumptions. Questioning boundaries often unlocks more creative solutions.

Why do we sometimes ignore the obvious?

Arguments vary, but the wheel is generally accepted to have been in use from around 5,500 years ago, or 3,500 BC. Around 1,000 years later, c. 2,500 BC, perhaps the most advanced civilisation in the world was in Egypt. The Egyptians had been responsible for many great leaps forward: the invention of ink and papyrus, the creation of the calendar and myriad discoveries in medicine, mathematics and architecture, including famously, the pyramids of Giza.

While other cultures, notably in Europe, were well into their utilisation of the wheel, in Egypt – and even in the much later Mayan civilisation in Latin America – the wheel was known about, but utilisation was missing, absent.

Our modern view is that the ancient Egyptians were for millennia one of the most advanced civilisations in history; yet many do not know that they lacked the one invention often cited as changing the world more than any other. In fact, though perhaps somewhat difficult to believe, the Aztecs, Incas and Native American cultures were all introduced to the wheel relatively recently; with the arrival of the European colonialists in the 15th and 16th centuries (AD).

This is what *Challenge Assumptions* is all about. The wheel was unused by the Egyptians and central Americans because it wasn't suitable in their circumstances. Try riding a bike through deep sand, or through steep impenetrable jungle and you'll see what we mean. This story also challenges us to *See the Whole System*, because when your lens of focus is too narrow, transformative possibilities like the wheel seem impossible. Thinking in terms of your system helps to illuminate the blind spots that are hidden by silos.

Despite the terrain, once the Egyptians adopted the wheel, they never looked back. Proof that the right tool – even arriving late – can be transformative. For us, there are two resonant lessons here about why, when faced with an obstacle, we resist adopting a better solution. We see it within organisations on a regular basis.

The first is the phenomenon of the 'blind spot'. We can all have our blind spots, whether it's refusing to see anything bad in our partners and children or taking on too much and being unwilling to delegate work. Often, a blind spot is characterised as something that we don't see now but appears evident afterwards. Blind spots can be as dangerous for business as they are for driving. Remember how Kodak ignored the potential of digital photography (which it conceived), how Nokia and Blackberry undervalued the iPhone, or how Blockbuster ignored the threat of Netflix?

The second motivation that makes us ignore new inventions or solutions, is a perceived lack of ownership. 'We do things our way', will resonate with many of you, even though, logically speaking, there is no intrinsic value to it – it is a solely emotional argument that depends on what you are doing. This prejudice makes us overvalue our creations and devalue external solutions.

If there is one thing we can say with total confidence, it is that right now there will be at least one innovation, probably several, that your company (and ours too) is not adopting. Further, that in a few years' time it will be clear we should have. Why? Well, it might be that you are limited by your blind spot, or that you are wedded to your in-house solution. Being aware of these limitations helps you identify opportunities, create new markets, lower costs and generate additional efficiency.

Periodically ask yourself: 'What opportunities exist today that I may not be valuing?'. Expose yourself to new things; allow yourself to be open to new methods, ideas or strategies.

If we surround ourselves with people who think similarly to us, it will be difficult to attract other perspectives (on that note, if you can't find a solution that works, it is sometimes worth asking a child; their unfettered and unrestricted thinking can often surprise!).

Today the world is exponentially quicker than it was five and half thousand years ago. There are more threats (and more opportunities), and they come at you faster. The Egyptians managed to live well for almost 1,000 years without wheels, and the Latin Americans nearly 2,000. In this ever-changing world, can your business last without embracing new thinking? The Egyptians had centuries; you might only have the next quarter. How long can you plod on, without inventing your wheel?

6.7 Average doesn't exist – question everything

Benchmarks and averages can hide unique circumstances. Making generic comparisons can lull you into a false sense of security. Make sure you are clear whether average really applies in each scenario.

The concept of 'average' is a relatively recent one. In the old days, when confronted with contradictory measurements, scientists, mathematicians or astronomers (the largest users of maths) tended to try to ascertain what they thought was the best measurement and ignore the remainder. As Professor Stephen Stigler notes in *The Seven Pillars of Statistical Wisdom*, 'you can actually gain information by throwing information away'. A statistical principle that underpins the entire idea of averages.

That concept, until the invention of modern statistical analysis, would have seemed anathema to the minds of the day. Only when Adolphe Quetelet, a Belgian astronomer and pioneer of statistics, developed his approach to 'social physics' during the 19th century, did the concept truly take hold. Quetelet developed the idea of 'social physics' and began to use mathematical tools to understand the behaviour of groups of humans.

To illustrate the point, he observed that by looking at an average of some elements, one no longer needed to spend as much time with the raw data. For example, if 100,000 died in Brussels in a six-month period, one could either look at each death certificate to learn all their ages, or calculate the average, to find out likely life expectancy. 'Throwing away' the volume of work associated with interrogating all the records each time created a leap forward.

Nowadays, we are well used to using averages as tools to simplify an increasingly complex world. When we read that the weight, height or age of a population has increased, we instinctively know that we are being measured by averages. Buy a piece of clothing in 'Medium' and we are purchasing something that is not bespoke, as was customary for a long time, but is the average of the population.

Until 1835, averages were used almost exclusively by astronomers, as a way of minimising the errors that imperfect measuring instruments introduced into calculations. Using the average of many observations, the approximation of the true value was better than any single one. That year, Quetelet published a work in which he calculated average height and chest size for men. He later applied the same method to calculate marriage, crime and suicide rates.

The concept quickly and easily captured the imagination. It became used widely, with generally very positive consequences. For example, shortly afterwards, Florence Nightingale implemented better hospital management methods based on measured and compared results, saving many lives.

During the American Civil War, averages were fundamental for the Unionist army to distribute rations, weapons and uniforms. Custom tailoring was no longer practical when recruiting thousands. By measuring a sample and aggregating small, medium and large, each soldier had clothing that, without being perfect, worked for his size, allowing mass production. This practice passed into civil society and allowed chains of clothing stores to exist with affordable prices.

Given this success it had with standardisation, the American army adopted this practice as a philosophy. In 1926, when they designed the first combat aircraft, they measured a large sample of their pilots (height, weight, arm length) and built the cockpit to suit the average pilot.

In World War II, North American aviation results were not brilliant. Many more planes crashed than expected. Different recruitment or training methods were tried, without improvements. Then they looked at the design of the cockpit. Would the build of the average pilot of the 1940s or 1950s be different from the build of the average pilot of the 1920s? The short answer was yes.

But one of the researchers challenged the premise of the question and probed deeper, getting a longer and far more interesting answer – and there is a lesson here for us all. His name was Gilbert Daniels, and he was an air force recruit from Harvard, which he had attended after winning a prestigious scholarship for a paper on the use of plants in pharmacology, aged 17. He had been fascinated by plants as a child, and after leaving the Air Force, went on to live a full academic life, ending up as Director of the Hunt Botanical Garden at Carnegie Mellon (Mishra, 2023).

What he did in those few years at the Air Force though, had some impact. Having sampled thousands of pilots across ten body measurements, Gilbert Daniels concluded something unexpected: nothing matched anybody. The average pilot did not exist. In the end, while designing a cockpit based on the 'average' pilot, they spent almost 30 years making a cockpit that didn't really fit anyone. A cautionary tale for budgeting design and a direct call to *Challenge Assumptions*. Building models around a theoretical average means a risk you design processes and pricing strategies that don't fit.

The uncomplicated solution is found in most vehicles today: adjustable seats and steering wheels. If it is possible that an organisation as well-structured as the Army, and later the American Air Force, were capable of winning world wars, but incapable of questioning something as simple as the concept of the 'average', is it possible you might be doing the same?

To be fair, the belief that averages were sound was by now widespread. At the surface level, 'average' appears to work fine – and it can be useful. Like anything, the more successful and longer a tool, process, or philosophy has been in force, the more difficult – and the more sensible – it is to query.

These beliefs become limiting presuppositions, precluding other ideas or action. Since they are likely to have a ripple effect across teams, they can silently end up dictating supplier choices, especially if you are not *Seeing the Whole System*. Like budgets that become prisons, these assumptions can restrict decision-making in future if they are not challenged. Quetelet deserves to be remembered for introducing the concept of 'averages', and Daniels for the courage to call into question even the most useful tools in some contexts.

When an organisation is making big, strategic decisions about its current and future operations, there are some important questions to ask. What assumptions am I using to make this decision? Have these assumptions been reviewed and validated? How recently was that done? What internal or external factors will have changed since that review? If you have never really thought about your assumptions and never questioned average you should start today. Once you've reviewed your assumptions, the next step is to understand your level of discomfort with each of them. Start with the ones that cause you the most discomfort.

Try this:

Write down your three most strongly held assumptions about how spending is managed in your organisation. Frame them in the context of Cost, Value, Risk and Change.

For each, ask:

1 **Certainty:** How sure are you that the assumptions are correct?
2 **Comfort:** How happy are you to leave each assumption unchallenged?

High-comfort / low-certainty items are the biggest opportunities for improvement.

Human beings like to have confirmed what we already believe, so human nature tends to mean we will be much more demanding with contrary evidence than we will be with that which confirms our original thinking. Knowing that we are likely to do this means that we can force ourselves to be more rational with our decision-making.

Whether you validate or subvert your assumptions one thing is for sure – any organisation that goes through a thorough process of identifying and assessing its assumptions through a solid process of continuous questioning will be better than those that do not – on average.

6.8 Dealing with resistance to change

Even necessary changes trigger resistance, fear of loss, fatigue from past failures and uncertainty about the future. Acknowledge resistance openly, communicate clearly and co-create solutions.

Darwin reminds us it is not the strongest of the species that survive, nor the most intelligent, but the ones most responsive to change. Change is inevitable, but there is something about making changes in a business, especially in areas that encroach on what people consider their personal domain, that tends to provoke a strong response.

The bark, however, is almost always far worse than the bite, in that the perception of change can loom larger than change itself. Being thoughtful regarding the timing and communication to relevant staff certainly helps. In some areas, changes can be implemented easily and seamlessly, and this can even be the case in relatively complex areas, if managed well.

Planning, communication and execution all matter, and you should be prepared to manage both the technical and the psychological aspects of the transition. People will have both irrational and legitimate concerns. You should manage the human response to the irrational and allow a voice to staff during the transformation process to allow them to input and, where possible, impact some of the decision-making. Where concerns exist regarding specification, quality, reliability and potential disruption, address them directly and allow time for people both to test the new products in production and get used to the idea mentally.

Bring them on board with a compelling story for why the changes are taking place, the benefits the changes can bring to the business or production process and what the changes will mean for them and their role. Don't forget your customers and ensure you have a robust and consistent story to tell all your partners. Train your relevant staff, if necessary, on how to work with the new supplier, but minimise this where it is uncomplicated – don't use a sledgehammer to crack a nut. Implementation of any new supplier involves a degree of risk, but planning, communication and executing well minimise it. Contingency plans should be in place to deal with any implementation issues or gaps in supply.

One major reason that implementations fail is that people budget only for the cost of the project. You must build in the *Cost of Change* too; budgeting for the 'how' as well as the 'what' can make or break success. Many incorrectly assume that change management refers to a defined period, a finite window, by the end of which all changes must be completed, before adhering to the new routines. In fact, change management is constant, continuous improvement.

Regular reviews should be conducted and reported, where opportunities to improve cost, quality or service should be assessed. Creation and ongoing monitoring of Key Performance Indicators (KPIs) is important, but do not let meetings drift into wasted time of flicking through endless sets of green traffic light icons. If you are hitting your KPIs all the time, then your plans could reveal a lack of ambition, rather than success. Reset constantly to do better; your metrics should reveal friction as well as glide – you need real visibility to see under the hood.

But don't just look at the numbers. Listen to your employees too. It is no good hitting targets if you fail to realise that half of your best engineers are thinking about leaving because process has become untenable. Asking for feedback to gauge the success of changes can also lead to new ideas and suggestions from your team. While we are on that subject, retain a good relationship with your supplier and ensure you are talking about ideas, innovation and new products with them too.

This should all be driven by the company leadership. We have mentioned the importance of communication, and this needs to come from the top. Employees across the board – but especially all levels of affected staff – should be clearly told, with appropriate advance warning, at least what will happen, even if they are not fully consulted.

Leaders should inhabit the behaviours they would like to see in their employees. This includes listening to feedback, being willing to adapt and being committed to the success of any changes. Building a culture that is change-ready requires ongoing effort. As we've learned, leading that change can be a high-wire act. It requires poise and preparation. Leaders can help by creating training and development opportunities for staff to help them build the skills they need, recognising and rewarding those who embrace new leadership roles and contribute to the success of any large-scale changes.

Managing change effectively depends on the scale of change. When it is complicated and difficult, plan longer, staff it better, create contingencies and allow more time. When it's easy, do not overdo it. In general, people like living inside their comfort zones, and change feels unwelcome. You need a culture that embraces change, innovation, creativity and fun. Look upon change not as having to adjust something that doesn't work for you but as an opportunity solve problems that don't yet exist.

Back in our principles chapter, we warned: when you don't *Control the Cost of Change*, change controls you. Take control before that happens.

6.9 Revolution vs evolution

What seem like revolutionary breakthroughs are usually the results of steady, incremental improvements. When continuous improvement becomes habit, innovation gains altitude and the sky becomes the limit.

At the turn of the twentieth century, there was a race for the sky. Teams all over the developed world were aiming upwards and training their sights on powered flight. Most of us will know that the race was eventually won by the Wright Brothers, Wilbur and Orville, of Dayton, Ohio in the US. But did you know, that at the time, not too many would have backed them to become the famous aviation pioneers they are known as today?

Rivals included a gathering of excellent and qualified engineers and scientists, led by the distinguished Samuel Pierpoint Langley of the Smithsonian Institute. They managed to get heavy funding from the American War Department as well as the Smithsonian. The major newspapers of the time followed their progress and tests with close interest, and they were considered the forerunners.

If there is a recipe for innovation, they had it all: the team, the funding and the motivation to make history. Yet Langley's team was beaten by two unknown high school dropouts, working as bike mechanics from their garage.

On 17 December 1903, the Wright brothers achieved powered flight and wrote their names in history. 'The Wright Flyer' featured a 12-horsepower gasoline powered engine driving twin propellers, in a bi-plane design and flew four times, achieving 260 metres on its fourth and what turned out to be its final flight. It crashed on landing and broke up. Later restored by Orville, this powerful symbol of freedom and a whole new world in the skies can now be seen on display at the National Air & Space Museum in Washington DC. Astronauts paid tribute to their predecessors by taking a piece of wood and some muslin torn from a wing of the Wright Flyer to the moon, tucked away in the pocket of Neil Armstrong's spacesuit.

The Wright Brothers first flight came just 9 days after Langley's failed attempt. The first flight may not have been long, but it signposted the way to a revolution in the way we travel. Over the next century, human civilisation moved forward at a pace hitherto unseen. The aviation industry was no exception and in many ways was leading the race. As the hope and optimism of powered flight gave way to the horrors of the First World War, the industry kept pace, from a jump of 260 metres by the Wright Brothers in 1903, to reconnaissance, bombers and fighter aircraft all being actively deployed in the war that started just 11 years later. With innovation necessary, the pace of the advance was astonishing. Even the transition to space travel and landing on the moon in the next 66 years is also astounding. And it's why the astronauts paid tribute to those pioneers.

As the 20th century continued to gather momentum after the Second World War, the world began to open. Both people and ideas spread far more quickly than before as air travel became increasingly affordable for the masses. We saw the rise of the corporation during the 20th century. Nearly all innovations today – from space travel to software, from cancer research to car safety features – involve large teams and substantial funding.

But is also remarkable to see, more than 100 years after the Wright Brothers' success, that there are still many cases where companies have gone on to become behemoths that started, just like the Wright Brothers, in their garages. Walt Disney and Mattel as well as Google, Microsoft, Dell and Amazon all started life in a garage. And these are just the giants. Although R&D does not guarantee success and, despite these origin stories, Google still spent $39.5 billion dollars on it in 2022 and Amazon a whopping $73.2 (Wikipedia, 2025).

Impossible numbers to imagine. Between the two companies, you'll find the figure of $66 billion, the total ad spending on social media by *all* US companies in 2022 (Statista, 2025). By comparison, these R&D spends are astonishing figures. Unless you happen to oversee R&D at one of those companies, the chances are that you do not have billions of dollars to invest in evolution.

But giving up on innovation means endangering your future. Lots of innovation ends in failure and it is all too easy to pass it off as a waste of money. Testing inevitably means failures. But nor can you only focus on one thing. True revolutions are hard to come by and necessarily rare. They take up space in our imaginations because they are exceptional. These advances operate as beacons for large companies with big budgets to attract the best talent.

But whether you have huge funding or minimal, there is a subtler way to generate advantage and progress in your business. Evolution. Not grand gestures, but investments in capability, systems and people that *Spend to Strengthen* your business, allowing each step to build on the last. Each step is taken with purpose and with clear direction to bring about meaningful change and development.

Wilbur and Orville Wright created the first successful powered aircraft, but they did not invent the propeller mechanism, the engine or the bi-plane design. They stood on the shoulders of giants and developed existing ideas to create their success. Since the creation of their flying machine, the aviation industry has developed to produce Concorde, the Airbus A380, the F35 fighter, the Space Shuttle and SpaceX's Starship rockets.

These creations are the result of incremental advances in a wide range of different fields, from aeronautics and navigation, to engineering, physics and cosmology. In a way, the Wright Brothers' revolution was only in creating the three-axis control system that allows the pilot to steer and maintain equilibrium. The basic tenet of this system remains the standard way of exerting control on all fixed wing aircraft, to this day. In aerodynamics, they perfected the work of previous pioneers, to whom they recognised their debt. Their success was the culmination of many previous small steps, coupled with a breakthrough, which allowed their revolution to take flight.

Many other small steps were needed to make aviation viable and many more until it became common and affordable. The aviation industry works well as an example of the most common way in which perceived revolutions only really became possible because of constant evolution. Infinite small steps create the conditions where a breakthrough can revolutionise an industry.

When a company decides to actively walk the path to improvement, these steps will create momentum, accumulate and compound. Not all change should come with a round of applause. Momentum built incrementally and purposefully can prove more resilient than any one-off revolution. Small steps represent 99% of any improvement process, yet they do not get the attention or recognition they deserve. A relentless pursuit of continuous improvement in all areas of the business (sales, R&D, purchasing, production, accounting, human resources, etc.) is bound to produce outstanding companies, as long as they remain humble and willing to accept that the best contributions can come from anywhere – a competitor, a consultant, a company from a completely different sector.

Perhaps you can imagine yourself as Wilbur or Orville Wright. In many ways, managing a company can be compared to flying an aircraft. You must push hard to even get it up in the air. Once you've achieved that, you cannot relax. You must keep your engines running and be aware of all internal and external controls, data and details. You need to ensure that the many components of the aeroplane are running smoothly and that your passengers are safe and happy. You must also be alert to external pressures, storms or violent changes in direction. Coping with the changing environment is essential.

Cost management projects need to be a major part of any organisation's efforts toward operational efficiency. To keep that aircraft flying high, you must shed unnecessary weight. And who knows, go into your garage from time to time, you might just find there has been enough evolution for your 'eureka!' moment.

6.10 50% of projects fail – so employ a robust model

Cost initiatives fail due to vague goals, poor governance and lack of follow-through. But discipline, accountability, structured reviews and rigorous execution give a far greater chance of success.

As we've already seen, having a plan is all very well and good, but if it's not underpinned by the correct thinking in the first place, it's fallible. *Spend with Purpose* and *Enough is a Strategy* both remind us to consider whether something is worth doing at all. If a decision is made to go ahead with a cost review project, you should work to give it the best chance to succeed.

All too often, legitimate initiatives are derailed by bad planning, or poor follow-through. What constitutes the opposite, and how do you give your project its best chance of success?

Reliable data on project success is scarce, but there's one source we return to. According to former World Champion Project Manager Antonio Nieto-Rodriguez's LinkedIn article (Nieto-Rodriquez, 2021), data from researchers' Standish Group found that only 35% of projects can be considered successful.

Clearly this ranges enormously depending on circumstance, sector, type of project, experience and myriad other factors. Plenty of other august institutions such as Bain & Co, McKinsey and HBR have all reported similarly. In other words, failure is normal. Those that avoid it know what to look for and plan flexibly. Contingencies are important, but in a cost management project, nothing is more important than accurate specification. Without it, you can plan all you want and it will still go south.

Remember, everything that you are spending should be reviewed through the lens of our smarter spending principles and aligned with the organisation's goals. If you think within these guidelines – allowing for common sense flexibility where necessary – you're more likely to actively prevent failure.

Communication – the invisible failure

What can't you see on a Gantt chart? You can't see the communication that underpins the plan. Get it wrong in the beginning and you can lose before planning even starts. Before the first tasks are assigned, there should be shared clarity of purpose – otherwise even good planning will go in the wrong direction. Planning shouldn't happen in silos anyway, but if it does, there is less likely to be misunderstandings if priorities are already aligned.

Beware this lack of shared context and clarity at planning stage, and beware too of unspoken assumptions 'procurement will get it for x price when the time comes', 'we will get the funding agreed' etc. Too many people nod through meetings, unable to admit that they don't understand the plan, the data or the strategy. Watch out for these people and communicate with them until they are clear. When it comes to clear communication, try and ditch the jargon. Avoid terms that can be misread or misinterpreted. Don't distort messaging by attempting to soften the blow or delay matters by softening risk.

Map who needs to know what and when. Build in communication plans and contingencies into the plan, not as an afterthought. Most mistakes and failures are not dramatic – they are often quiet but catastrophic misunderstandings – like the US & UK space teams mixing up imperial and metric measurements.

What makes a model 'robust'?

Any plan is better than not having one at all, but a bad plan can be dangerous. As we mentioned, having a robust plan is not the same as being rigid. It should be flexible, stress-tested and visible to stakeholders. It should *See the Whole System*, considering the consequences, goals, risk, roles, responsibilities and accountability of everyone involved.

Plan for implementation and training and budget for both. Remembering that we must *Control the Cost of Change* to achieve the objectives – if you are not doing this, you may as well just guess. Considered planning can be a matter of life and death. There is a clear difference between the costly mess that was the Charge of the Light Brigade during the Crimean War and the meticulously planned success of D-Day in WWII.

Perhaps your savings project doesn't carry the same weight of risk and responsibility, but you can still learn how to get it right far more often that 35% of the time. Love them or hate them, Amazon have demonstrated how extremely effective their tight feedback-driven model can be. It balances frugality with experimentation and their 'two-pizzas' team size and written memo culture both help prevent project failures.

Robust planning models have communication built in by design

- Daily huddles or weekly stand-ups
- Pre-mortems and post-mortems
- Shared dashboards / spend visibility
- Clear escalation protocols
- Decision logs or 'what we know' summaries

What gets in the way?

- **Busyness culture** – Nobody has time to do anything properly, so processes become weaker, standards slip and vital jobs don't get done. See the Grenfell Tower tragedy and subsequent UK cladding crisis.
- **Fear of visibility / accountability** – 'If I don't take responsibility, I cannot be blamed if it fails'. See the UK Post Office's failure to see that the financial

discrepancies it accused Postmasters of were due to IT issues, and not the sudden dishonesty of hundreds of loyal workers.

- **Planning without feedback loops** – No good the Boeing executives reacting to the Max crisis by supressing feedback from engineers. A post-mortem 6 months later isn't feedback, it's an autopsy. When feedback is delayed or ignored, plans self-destruct.
- **No clear owner** – Role confusion can lead to 'we will figure it out'. But when you are trying to do that against a deadline, sometimes you just run out of road. Without accountability some things just don't get finished.

By contrast we can point to Toyota's production system, the success of NASA's Apollo programme and those Normandy landings for proof that when comms are good, contingencies are in place and nothing is left to chance, plans can work. But only if you put the work in. Planning is also a form of investment – of time, effort and money. All the things we spend can be considered using the principles from this book. As with money, plan to spend your time and effort deliberately, with intention – and remember that Lincoln quote about sharpening the axe. Planning badly can damage your reputation – as it has the UK Post Office and building industry.

Like those mundane daily communication failures, usually planning doesn't fail because people don't care. It fails because good intentions are ambushed by hidden dependencies, vanishing data and shifting priorities. That's why a robust model doesn't just help you succeed. It helps you to survive. When models are used with rigour and adaptability, they do more than deliver results. They have the power to de-risk failure itself. A robust plan won't guarantee success, but it will protect you from chaos. Without one, even the best teams, technologies, or intentions can fail. With one, you can build a project that bends before it breaks.

6.11 Don't design for failure

Many programmes are set up to fail safely: too cautious to create impact, not bold enough to be transformative. Designing for success means committing resources and leadership attention. Half-measures only waste time and goodwill.

Imagine two high-speed trains, 6 kilometres apart on the same track, accelerating in opposite directions and heading straight for each other. An imminent rail disaster, the horror of the potential for loss of life. But what if we told you that in this story, the trains had been set against each other deliberately? In 1896, William Crush, an employee of the Missouri Kansas Texas Railroad company, decided to make use of some old disused locomotive engines, by staging a deliberate crash as a spectacle.

No admission was charged, but train tickets were sold to a special station and quickly erected viewing stadium in the desert. They dug wells, erected special stands for the press and built circus stages and refreshment stalls. Expecting perhaps 25,000 people, 40,000 turned up. The event was delayed for an hour as police struggled with spectators to keep the 200-metre safety perimeter stipulated by organisers.

The teams from each train started their engines and, as they gathered speed, jumped from the locomotive. According to contemporary newspaper reports, the trains met with an almighty bang followed a moment of silence. Interrupted almost immediately by a further massive explosion as both boilers exploded simultaneously, firing shrapnel in all directions, some of it into the crowd.

As the panicked crowd dispersed, people were hit. Two died, a further six were seriously injured, including a photographer, Jarvis 'Joe' Deane, who lost an eye. William Crush was promptly fired. None of the experts who set the perimeter had imagined a boiler explosion, never mind both going up together. And nobody *Challenged Assumptions* about safe distancing, even if it sounds like the crowd and the police were a little spooked.

Foresight, planning and corporate responsibility must have been concepts that developed later. Now, we would question where the planning budget went. Even technical expertise can fail when it's not connected to consequences. When considering risk, your job is not to consider what is likely to happen, but what isn't likely, but possible.

The story reminds us of all those times in business where we can see systems that seemed designed to go wrong – that have failure built into the model – yet on we go. Almost all organisations will have ideas that were seized upon in the past and are now writ into company lore. They are just a fact, they are no longer discussed, and their value and purpose are never questioned or re-evaluated. As we've discussed, legacy decisions often become invisible and the longer they go unchallenged, the more entrenched they become, at least until some brave soul comes along. It's why we advocate for *Challenging Assumptions*, not annually, but habitually. When legacy decisions begin to petrify, they stop serving the organisation and start hurting it.

This is how wars start, how states support bankrupt companies and how elections are lost. The Watergate wiretaps, which caused Nixon's downfall, were decided on by a small group of people, oblivious not only to the risks, but to the fact that the risk was likely unnecessary, as he probably would have won the election even without listening in on his opponents.

We encourage a prior autopsy of the project, which essentially means asking today 'imagine that we are a year on, discussing why the project failed. What would we be saying?'. Depending on what arises, the plan can be revoked, reviewed, or the most damaging potential mitigated.

In Texas, in 1896 a few minutes after the boilers exploded, the crowd began to return to the scene, eager to collect souvenirs of the disaster. In terms of what we now call PR, despite the deaths, the media were kind and for the organisers, overall, the event ended up going well, even after they paid out compensation. William Crush was even reinstated the following day.

No doubt the two people who died wish the autopsy had taken place beforehand, rather than being required afterwards. In companies, the price of wrong assumptions is seldom the loss of life, though the Grenfell tragedy proved it can be. Whatever you trade in, make sure you are always *Challenging Assumptions*. When a potential disaster is staring you in the face, act. Act to get your people safe and away from the blast zone, should your next mistake detonate.

References

Harari, Y.N. (2017) *Homo Deus: A Brief History of Tomorrow*. Harper.

Mishra, P. (2023) Gilbert Daniels: The gardener who changed our world. Available at https://punyamishra.com/2023/04/14/gilbert-daniels-the-gardener-who-changed-the-world/ (last accessed 4 December 2025).

Nieto-Rodriguez, A. (2021) 14#: Everlasting poor project success rates – how come? *LinkedIn*. Available at https://www.linkedin.com/pulse/14-everlasting-poor-project-success-rates-how-come-nieto-rodriguez (last accessed 4 December 2025).

Stigler, S. (2016) *The Seven Pillars of Statistical Wisdom*. Harvard University Press.

Statista (2025) Social network advertising spending in the United States from 2021 to 2025 (in billion U.S. dollars). Available at https://www.statista.com/statistics/736971/social-media-ad-spend-usa/?srsltid=AfmBOoqZq0lbUXH-QoxUhTfc04WCAsYjZnPyHgPOU1tJU36o3KnJQGp7U (last accessed 4 December 2025).

Wikipedia (2025). List of companies by research and development spending. Available at https://en.wikipedia.org/wiki/List_of_companies_by_research_and_development_spending (last accessed 4 December 2025).

chapter 7

The path to results

7.1 Always the same storm, just different boats

External disruption, like economic downturns, price spikes, or supply chain shocks, can have wildly different effects on organisations. The difference lies not in the storm itself but in the preparation of culture, systems and clarity. Build the resilience that lets you ride out whatever comes next.

The COVID pandemic and its consequences are perhaps the biggest disruption to the economy of our lives. A great storm that shook everything. If each company is a boat, we travel on different boats. Some seem to have been built exactly for these conditions and thrive in them; others are only lucky enough to withstand the storm. Many will suffer damage but survive, perhaps even stronger.

Within each of our organisations we can largely say that we are all in the same boat. If this feeling is shared, then resistance to change falls. This is why *Spending with Purpose* matters. When teams understand not just *that* change is coming, or *what* it is, but *why* it's happening, they are far more likely to align. Purpose isn't just about making strategic, or even ethical decisions, it's about getting every rower in the boat pulling in the same direction.

Before the coronavirus crisis, assuming costs were under control was bad (although very common), now it is a critical vulnerability. Cost control is not static – assumptions that felt safe before the storm may become liabilities. From experience we know, without any doubt, that all companies can reduce their costs without changing personnel. So where to start?

More than 100 years ago, when counting the peas produced in his small garden, a man discovered a strange relationship: around 80% of the peas came from 20% of the pods. Strangely, this coincided with another finding of his: that approximately 80% of the land in Italy belonged to 20% of the population. This gentleman was Vilfredo Pareto; we have already mentioned his 'law'. He was an economics professor and discovered that this 80/20 relationship persisted in a wide range of situations and historical contexts.

In costs too, the 80/20 rule generally applies, which is why starting by listing the costs in descending order and analysing the largest ones is one obvious way to start. We would also add another: highlighting some 'low-hanging fruit'. Starting a broad cost reduction project with wins, however easy, instils a shared sense of possibility and this early traction reinforces the fact that change is possible.

Even well-managed ships may sink. Having a culture of continuous questioning and improvement reduces the chances of being among the victims of a wreck. It is vital to have the humility to recognise that there is room for improvement and learning.

Fundamental to implementing a cost management culture is sharing the objectives with all employees, explaining why they are important for the common future and what you want to transform that future into. A clear vision motivates great ideas. Measuring and sharing the results achieved is the driver of continuity.

Storms expose weaknesses, but they also reveal strength. A smarter approach to spending helps your team to row in rhythm, not just surviving, but steering the right course.

7.2 Review specifications carefully

Poor specifications create hidden costs. Assess requirements thoroughly each time. True value starts with clarity; buy only what you really need and don't base future decisions on isolated bad experiences. Use data, not anecdotes.

As part of a cost optimisation project that we were developing for a client in the printing area, when visiting the incumbent supplier, a colleague of ours was astonished by the amount of waste being produced. Before being printed, the sheets were cut so that our client's catalogues had the specified measurements. When asked why there was so much waste, the supplier replied that the customer's requirements were there to be met, and he did so to the letter.

Working with the supplier, we discovered that if the catalogue were 1 mm less in height and 1.5 mm less in width, it would meet another paper producer's standard. With one simple conversation and a sensible decision, the entire cutting operation and all the associated waste were eliminated.

The result was a catalogue almost indistinguishable from the previous one. In fact, placing the two versions of the catalogue side by side, our client's marketing managers were unable to identify which was which, until we told them. As a result of a simple tweak, the supplier made substantial savings on their operations, which they were able to pass on to our customer.

This is just one example of many that illustrate the potential of what will probably be the least travelled path to cost reduction: reviewing specifications. The focus when purchasing goods or services is almost always on the quality / price binomial.

Too often this focus is even more on price than quality – ignoring *Value before Cost* because although the price is visible on the label, the quality may not be so easy to ascertain. When we only see the price tag, we undervalue the cost of rework, waste or below-par performance. All damage the brand. Specifications define value; mess it up and you'll fail before you've even started.

In the case we describe, the quality / price ratio was adequate and within reasonable limits, but we achieved significant savings by looking from another perspective and asking the question 'Is there another way to achieve the same result?'. This question, which should be asked loudly and often, opens a world of possibilities. Often, people who shout the loudest for this kind of change are dismissed as troublemakers, or attention seekers. In fact, they are often seekers of simplicity or can approach problems and recognise patterns in a different way, producing more effective processes or methods. This can help to demonstrate the value of having a neurodiverse workforce.

Looking at the goods and services consumed by companies with this lens, we soon find a series of examples of questions that could lead to results: Are the dimensions of the boxes we use really the most suitable for packaging our product and transporting it? Could they be thinner? Could they be thicker, or in another material, and be reused? Could we therefore fit more product on a pallet, producing compounded savings? Can we use used or rental pallets? What if it's not for everything, but just for a certain product or customer segment? Will paying more for insurance with a low deductible really make sense? What if we increase the deductible, assuming part of the risk? What is *Enough*, and what is overkill? Where is the Goldilocks zone?

When it comes to insurance, both at a business and personal level, its objective should be to let us sleep well, knowing that we will not face situations of extreme financial shock. It therefore makes perfect sense, for most people or companies, to take out insurance that covers potential significant losses. For most people this means their house or car: for companies, their facilities, workers, or risks arising from their activity.

This detail about the insurance market serves to frame a question along the lines of those we asked previously, which could be: does taking out this insurance really make sense? If the answer is an unequivocal 'yes', proceed, but there are other cases in which the answer should be a resounding 'no'.

While helping one of our clients, we saw that they had zero excess insurance for all company vehicles, meaning that if they had any accident, scratch or dent they would not pay anything. Such insurance is quite expensive, as it takes away the responsibility of those who take it out. This cohort then tends to place more claims on the insurance, therefore increasing the bill for everyone who opts for this solution.

In a case like this, it would make a lot more sense to have an excess, even a high one, and save on the insurance premium. In the event of an accident, we pay up to a point and the insurance company pays from there. In the long term, and for a fleet, it will usually be the best option, even if in one particularly unlucky year, it may not be.

Just as we saw with the 'average' pilot that doesn't exist, treating all risks – or specifications – the same is a category error. Each decision needs individual scrutiny. You must *See the Whole System* and must balance risk and reward too, just as the insurer does. Naturally, in this case we recommended that our client opt for higher deductibles when it comes to cars, but to use part of the savings to take out a sensible civil liability policy.

7.3 Beware of automatic renewals

> *Automatic renewals are one of the most common sources of waste. Contracts quietly roll over, often at higher prices or with unnecessary scope, undermining cost discipline. Build in reviews and treat each renewal as a deliberate choice.*

We all know the story of Troy and the Greek wooden horse. The fall of Constantinople in 1453 was also resolved by a piece of leftfield thinking. Sultan Mehmed II, of the Ottoman empire, already buoyed by the development of cannon-fire, laid siege to Constantinople for 55 days, bombarding the wall's weakest sections.

It was Mehmed's decision to get his army to walk warships across a parcel of land in the dead of night though, that really turned the tide. By depositing them in the Golden Horn they acquired primacy on the water. The Venetians' that had been helping Constantinople resupply were forced back and within days, the city belonged to the Ottomans.

A little later, in 1519, the Aztec empire was at the height of its power. Similarly, when Spanish Conquistador Hernán Cortés landed on Central American shores, he managed to persuade Aztec emperor Montezuma that they were not a threat and was welcomed into their court, before Tenochtitlán, the Aztec capital, fell to the Spanish.

All these cases are mentioned here to illustrate the dangers of welcoming something or someone seemingly benign in with open arms. What might look perfectly reasonable today can change quickly, and we see heavy risks hidden in contractual conditions, particularly in service contracts.

The auto-renewal provision is a defining characteristic of many of the contracts we encounter in our day-to-day lives. On the face of it, a service contract with an auto-renewal term seems reasonable. After all, as the client, you would not want any break in service, nor would you want service to drop off the cliff at the end of a contract. Indeed, if you are satisfied today, why not let it rollover indefinitely? You can always rescind when things change.

In our experience, there tend to be all sorts of hidden – or even visible but underscrutinised – terms and conditions associated with ongoing service contracts. These can sometimes function as a kind of Trojan Horse, allowing the suppliers to gain access to your custom at different rates, or with different expectations as the contract continues. Often these ongoing terms are different, and they have the power to dig deeply into your costs, long term.

Hidden risk and cost creep thrive in the shadows, so *Build for Visibility* is important here, whether being conscious of auto-renewal clauses, annual price increases or rebate clauses. If you can't see these clearly, you can't plan for them properly and they'll end up boxing you into a corner. Many contracts renew with the same period as the initial term – another 1, 3 or 5 years. On top of that, the exit period may seem ample, 90 days for instance. Often though, over time, this 90-day period gets 'lost' and when you remember, it's already too late to do anything about it.

In most companies, indirect or overhead costs are not deemed as high worth as others, and are often 'on autopilot' and therefore are not really thought about too much. If and when someone has some time available to investigate them, there is a high probability it will not coincide with the best period to negotiate terms. These delays reveal a deeper issue. *Control the Cost of Change* isn't just about implementation, but preparation. If the right time to change isn't planned into the system, the organisation ends up locked into legacy costs.

Worse still, auto-renewals often trigger contractual provisions related to pricing. These may include reversion to 'default rate pricing' for a service or can often be pegged to a fixed percentage uplift or indexation. These are usually substantially higher than what is available in the market at the time.

Sometimes, these contracts allow for the supplier to announce new pricing just before renewal, giving a short period – two weeks, for instance – for the client to quickly find a new solution with an alternative supplier and give notice. The alternative of course, as all suppliers know – is that the client will do nothing, and therefore businesses find themselves just implicitly accepting those new terms. This 'implied consent' can then affect pricing for 1, 3, or even 5 years.

Often, suppliers will send these new price communications at specific times of year, when they know focus and attention from their clients are low. For example, communications with short deadlines are often sent during holiday periods, where they may linger on someone's desk or in their email for days or weeks. When they are noticed, it is too late.

It is generally accepted that it costs somewhere between 5 and 7 times more to acquire a new customer than to retain an existing one. Attracting new customers involves expenses related to marketing, advertising and sales efforts. Therefore, it makes total sense for the seller to include auto-renewal conditions in every contract. It makes much less sense for the customer to accept them, so this is where you *Challenge* ***their*** *Assumptions*. Just because it's an industry norm for them, doesn't mean it serves your goals. Inactivity is not a plan, and default contract terms are usually favoured by the authors.

What can we do to avoid this trap?

If you have strong bargaining power, you can just demand that it disappears altogether, or that after the initial term it renews for a rolling 30 days, rather than a longer contract with a specific exit period. That provides you all the benefits of no breaks in service, without the downside. When the contract is an acceptance one, set in stone, as many utilities and telecom contracts are, you still have options: the most obvious is to mark on your calendar a reminder to review the situation ahead of time.

This, however, has a few obvious disadvantages. The first is that while your calendar 1, 3 or 5 years from now will appear empty, the reality is you will be busy again with ongoing work by the time that period rolls around. Other priorities crowd it out.

Another is that technology may fail, either because a new system was installed or some data is lost during the intervening period, and the reminder disappears. Another still is that the individual responsible may have moved. Either they will have changed role, where that responsibility no longer falls under their remit, or they may have left the company, and their replacement won't have that reminder in place.

One of our colleagues that previously worked for a telecommunications supplier told us about a client who had a clever method to deal with this situation, which essentially passes the responsibility back. Whenever they signed a new contract with an auto-renewal clause, they always wrote, signed and delivered a termination letter for the same deadline alongside that contract, with a mention that they expected the service to be continued under the same conditions, until a new contract was made, either with the same or another supplier.

After all, if you have a 90-day notice period, it means 'at least 90 days'. You can deliver it at any time before the period as well as during it, including, if you want to, 5 years before. It counts just the same. This kind of forward thinking really reflects *Spend with Purpose*, as well as *Build for Visibility* and *See the Whole System*. By putting even mundane administrative and operational tasks into the planning, you are embedding deliberate, proactive decision-making into your future.

It's so simple to integrate, and it's not about price but being in control. Our colleague told us that, as a supplier, this kept him on his toes, as he was painfully aware he could lose that client at renewal. Although very few people use this strategy, it might just be the best one we've come across to counter the tricks hidden inside these clauses.

7.4 The most expensive umbrella in the world

Failing to plan creates avoidable expense. Urgency drives poor decisions, and small lapses repeated often become material costs.

On Orchard Street in Preston, Lancashire, stood Goodwin Brothers umbrella shop (now closed sadly). The slogan, embossed into the stonework on the shop (and still visible) was 'We shall have rain'. Despite seeing this advice often, when patronising the pub next door (the only one in the country with an entrance on three different streets!), Neil has left the house without an umbrella, only to be caught out by the rain more than once.

We have all left the house and forgotten the umbrella, just to be caught out by heavy rain. Pedro less frequently in Portugal, but still. Sometimes you will pass a shop that sells umbrellas and buy a cheap £5 one, just to get to where you are heading relatively dry (after all, you have one at home). Less than 10 minutes later, your purchase catches the wrong gust of wind and is bound for the bin. £5 is not an enormous amount of money, but the story illustrates one of our ten principles. The perfect reminder of *Value before Cost*. They are not equal. The price of the umbrella was low, but the average cost per use was substantial. A flimsy purchase like that comes in at about £30 per hour, yet you arrive drenched anyway. Not great return on investment.

The point is this: price is not value, and cost is not just what's on the tag.

While we're talking about getting wet, let us also remind you of the Vimes Boot Index of socioeconomic unfairness. From the *Discworld* novels by the late Sir Terry Pratchett, the theory is named for Sam Vimes, Captain of the Ankh-Morpork city watch.

It affirms that people in poverty must buy cheap, low-quality products that need to be replaced repeatedly, proving more expensive in the long run than more expensive items. In the second novel in the series, Vimes opines on how expensive it is to be poor.

> *'The reason that the rich were so rich, Vimes reasoned, was because they managed to spend less money. Take boots, for example. ... A man who could afford fifty dollars had a pair of boots that'd still be keeping his feet dry in ten years' time, while a poor man who could only afford cheap boots, would have spent a hundred dollars on boots in the same time and would still have wet feet'.*
>
> *(See Wikepedia, 2025)*

We see this a lot. Buying the cheapest machinery, parts, computers, or vehicles is a false economy, but 'lowest price is the best decision' thinking can be pervasive. In Vimes' case poverty was *forcing* him into making what he knows is a bad decision. In business, we often fall into the same trap *voluntarily*. I bet you have bought something cheap that fell apart. It is annoying, but what really hurts is if this happens when spending premium money.

We've dealt with 'expensive must mean good'. Let's look at another one of these myths: that brand, or reputation equals quality. In 2020, a poll in Auto Express ranked Kia second only to Lexus for fewest reported problems (Jervis, 2025). Mercedes-Benz? 28th out of 30. Consumer Reports placed Kia 9th (Kominek, 2020). Mercedes? 20th. Are we saying Kia is better than Mercedes?

No, we're just saying reputation can last beyond virtue and it's important to examine what you want. It's easy to compare prices, hard to compare quality. Harder still to define it. Expectations vary. Requirements change. When you're buying unfamiliar items, especially in areas outside your expertise, the default setting is guesswork.

That's where total cost of ownership (TCO) helps. It looks beyond sticker price to include maintenance, training, set-up, energy use, upgrades and more. TCO is not a perfect scientific formula, but even rough TCO thinking can save you a fortune. A £20 umbrella lasting 5 years delivers value. A £5 purchase lasting 10 minutes would not. And that cost wasn't just financial: it included inconvenience, wasted time and a soaked walk. Of course, some of this is behavioural.

Spot your comfort strategy

Start by *identifying your defaults.*

People buying outside their comfort zone often fall back on shortcuts. For the last business purchases you made – which of these did you default to?

- Buy the cheapest: low risk, right?
- Buy the most expensive: must be the best, surely?
- Pick the middle one: it's safe.

Next, reflect on your experience

- How well did the decision play out?
- What assumptions were you making about price and performance?
- Did you feel confident because of price – or tangible evidence?

Finally, rethink your decision – the Smarter way

- Define your needs clearly
- Compare only options that genuinely meet those needs
- Estimate the total cost of ownership, including any friction and your effort
- Apply *Enough is a Strategy,* to only buy what delivers value.

How might your choice have changed?

These 'comfort strategies' persist because they sometimes work. That makes them dangerous. A £5 umbrella might last 5 years. A £20 one might break in a week. But relying on luck is not a strategy. We've talked about equating price with performance. In another study, the same energy drink helped people solve more puzzles, but only when they believed it cost more (Shiv, 2005).

Most SME buyers aren't trained professionals. They're heads of departments buying as part of a wider role. That's ok. But it means you'll sometimes find yourself in unfamiliar waters. When you do, avoid the trap of lazy decision-making. Don't assume cheap is safe. Don't assume expensive is better. Don't assume the middle is wise.

I am sure many of us bought a cheap car when we were younger, only to be paralysed by repair and maintenance costs. Think. Compare. Plan. Ask for help if needed. You can learn to buy better. Smarter spending success isn't just about saving money; it's about not throwing it in the bin.

7.5 Why you should call an expert

Using consultants or specialists is a strategic choice, not a weakness. External perspective helps organisations see blind spots. Trying to do everything internally can be expensive and selective help can be the fastest path to results.

We are conscious that we are cost management consultants. As such, we understand that writing some lines about why you should call an expert might be akin to 'never ask a barber if you need a haircut'. Still, this point needs to be made. But we'll make it one of the shortest chapters in the book.

Common sense tells us it is impossible for any company to justify having a specialist buyer on staff in every area that they spend money: one who knows both sides of the table, who has worked many years in the industry they are now buying from. Even in the largest companies, we know of none that employ specialist purchasing professionals in every category, including every overhead, or indirect cost area. It does not make good economic sense to do so. Yet it is also true that when one buyer covers multiple cost areas; it leads to blind spots, especially in complex areas or those – like overheads – that are often mostly left in the dark anyway.

You would need to have in your purchasing team people who have worked many years in logistics companies, then the same for IT & telecoms, packaging, energy, fuels, insurance, office supplies, card payment fees etc. Some larger organisations will employ buyers to cover indirect costs, but even they tend only to have a small team – and typically not one person per area. In most cases these buyers come from their industry, rather than the sector the suppliers occupy.

Even in those rare cases where that happens, after a few years living in your reality, the buyers' benchmark of the overall market will inevitably erode, and these teams lack the capacity to check these areas regularly enough. That's a failure to *Spend with Purpose* – when spend becomes routine, it loses its strategic value. We would also make the distinction between a specialist and a specialist *buyer.*

We've said your IT Director is a specialist. They have specialist knowledge in IT that enables them to fulfil their role and responsibilities. In this example – though you can apply this to operations, office management, insurance and the rest – the IT Director already has a long list of duties they must succeed in to perform their job. On top of that, they are also given the IT budget – these days usually a significant sum – and expected to deliver best value to the business.

However, the experience that got them the job, does not often – or ever – include purchasing and procurement training. Instead, they are expected to assume those responsibilities on top of all those others.

Purchasing is a skill. An understanding of the supply market is essential. You should be *Spending to Strengthen* your capabilities here. Specialist knowledge of suppliers and their capabilities is essential if you want to derive optimum value from the market and invest in the future. This means getting the best possible products and services for the best possible price from the best supplier for your needs.

Experience matters. While both bring something to the table, you wouldn't trust an ear, nose and throat (ENT) surgeon with your heart, and you wouldn't ask an aircraft engineer to fix your car. Someone who is an IT *procurement* specialist – whose job, every day, is to derive best value from the market – will be better at achieving best value than someone who is an IT specialist, without purchasing training, who does it as a small percentage of their job.

Decathletes are good, but a 100-metre sprinter, or a javelin thrower can run faster, and throw further. Practice makes perfect. Carry on using your own employees to buy but recognise that their success will be limited in comparison to what is possible. What is possible is better bang for your buck, and a wider profit margin. That's exactly what senior leadership needs. As we know from *Profit Fuels Progress*, margin is not just a number, it's freedom to invest, compete and sustain and as a company director, your job is to maximise the value of the business. That's it. We promised we would keep it short.

7.6 Only data provides clarity

Evidence-based decisions require more than good intentions. Do not mistake anecdotes and partial truths for insight. Clarity depends on rigorous data and the humility to question what you believe you already know.

The saying 'If you can't measure it, you can't manage it', attributed to quality guru W. Edwards Deming has become popular. We prefer another Deming quote: 'In God we trust, everyone else must show us the data'. We're *Building for Visibility*, or we're in the dark, where leading becomes guessing.

Both phrases reveal the importance of complete information about the business for decision-making. In companies, the main source of management information is, or should be, their accounting, as all their activity is recorded there. However, accounting often suffers from just being a legal imperative and not a useful management tool.

If accounting only exists to meet legal requirements you're missing the potential of a big strategic lever. For it to be truly useful, it is necessary that it:

1 be current – information that is more than a week old is like watching old movies: interesting, but of little practical use to most businesses
2 is structured in such a way as to easily answer our questions
3 generates reports that are readable by a non-accountant
4 groups information into large relevant categories that can be 'drilled down' into smaller categories for more detailed analysis when necessary.

It also seems easier to measure the sales side of the business (whether expressed in pounds, units, absolute margin, or percentage) than the costs side. The main reason is that modern data standards allow most companies to track every sale to the penny. But ask what they spend on packaging, telecoms or logistics and things suddenly get a little vague.

Focussing on the costs side of the equation, what do *x* litres of diesel for a company car and a Zoom call have in common? Both are legitimate means of reaching a customer. Sometimes, only being there will work. But we know that one has a substantially higher cost than the other: financial and environmental.

In a world where companies are increasingly being held to account for their impact, what questions should we now be asking about the way in which decisions such as these consume the company's resources? In circumstances like these, companies should increasingly be thinking about what is '*Enough*'.

Knowing what is essential to measure is important, but how do you decide what falls into this category? Here, the most recommended strategy is to follow the Pareto rule (designed for other purposes, but very useful in management). Knowing that 20% of the items represent 80% of the costs, the company should concentrate its key personnel on these 'core' costs to obtain the best results. For each significant cost item, ambitious objectives should be set and people who exceed them should be rewarded. When you have finished, you should restart the process.

The other 80% of the items still represent 20% of the costs, and these should not be ignored. It is still important to make sure that you are not wasting the money that costs so much to generate. Review them frequently, comparing them with market benchmarks or request the help of specialists, allowing staff to be freed up for tasks vital to the company's core business.

Implementing a demanding, cost-conscious culture, in which 'showing the data' is the rule, makes companies more competitive. Data-driven cultures help to drive purpose, impact, priorities and performance. 'We'll get round to thinking about it' is of little use. There is never an ideal moment, where your desk is suddenly clear – that will only happen if you go bankrupt – so start measuring what matters now.

7.7 Beware of sellers' tricks

Buyers buy from sellers. They have plenty of what Robert Cialdini calls 'weapons of influence' to use. We highlight them here, to ensure your decisions are grounded in value, not persuasion.

When a pride of lion hunts gazelle in the African savanna, what we are watching is the latest in a multi-generational arms race. Each lion is the descendant of a long line of winners. The animals that survived are those who got to catch enough prey to feed and reproduce. Each gazelle is also the descendant of a long line of winners: in their case, the animals that escaped predators long enough to live and leave behind offspring. As the ancestors of lions got stronger and faster, so did the gazelles, continuously responding to changes in their environment.

Most salespeople will recognise the continuous arms race between predators and prey. Sellers' tactics also evolve to catch us, and we must ensure we retain our purpose and not be reactive or manipulated in our decision-making. We saw in 'Most expensive umbrella' how easy it can be to default to safe decisions – cheapest, most expensive, middle – especially under pressure. But, as you learn to your cost, these shortcuts are risky.

In the old days, buyers often relied on information gained by meeting different salespeople. In recent years, the buying journey has changed. Buyers now have access to more information than ever about the products and services they need to procure. Sellers have lost control of part of the process and the information asymmetry that used to exist has diminished. The more the level of buyer sophistication increases, the more barriers are raised, meaning the abilities and arsenal of a good salesperson must also improve. A salesperson unable to adapt to the increasing level of their buyers will starve for business. Therefore, for the salesperson to survive, they too must adapt and enhance their skills.

We are going to share with you some of the strategies that salespeople use to help them to sign new clients and keep their margins healthy. Many of these are simply good business practice, though others can be somewhat manipulative. Either way, being aware that they exist may give you an advantage when it comes to negotiation and getting the best terms as a buyer.

To do this, we're going to provide a quick overview of Professor Robert Cialdini's 'six pillars' of persuasion, outlined in his book *Influence*, first published in 1984. Cialdini studied, and even sometimes infiltrated, organisations that were effective in sales.[1] The result was the identification of six weapons of influence, which we will briefly describe and relate to B2B sales.

1 Reciprocity

As part of our human nature, we feel obliged when offered something, to give something back in return. This happens because reciprocal agreements are part of the lubricant of social relationships.

If we have stopped and watched a good street performer, if we've been genuinely entertained, we will probably feel bad if we do not give them some money. in the same way, when a supplier gives us a gift, it often induces us into giving something back. We might accept a higher price or not look so thoroughly at their service faults after a nice day out at an event. Most of the time these are not even conscious acts. We will likely not even be aware that this is happening.

These offers might come as gifts, though most companies have policies that limit acceptance. It is certainly more prudent to think of these gifts as services

1 Curiously, the book is written mostly in a 'buyer beware' style, but in a later interview Cialdini said he had realised after the book was released that it was being read mostly by salespeople, and he was often paid to show them how they could use these principles to increase their sales.

the supplier is offering without charging for. It is clear you will be paying for them somewhere else in the contract.

Don't allow yourself to be knocked off course. Anchor decisions on defined need and measurable outcomes, not perceived pressure to meet in some arbitrary 'middle'. Suppliers may ask for an outrageous term (payment in advance, or delivery once a month), only to then retreat to just a small price increase, which you are now more accepting of by comparison.

The social cards are so stacked up against us whenever the reciprocity principle is used that it can be difficult to be immune.

There are, however, ways in which to mitigate its effects.

1 Understand when it is being used on you.
2 Defuse the bomb, by rejecting the free offer and demanding transparent pricing.
3 Analyse each subsequent offer on its merits, and not on what has gone before it .

2 Commitment and consistency

In his autobiography, John Cleese (of *Monty Python* and *Fawlty Towers* fame) says that in his short career as a schoolteacher, he attended several of his colleagues' classes. The contrast between two of them was huge. The first was a harsh and severe teacher; the other was funny and nice. Curiously, he realised the students preferred the former to the later.

The reason was that while the first teacher was always harsh and severe, the second's behaviour varied wildly. He was not consistent. When knowing what to expect, the students knew how to behave. When faced with inconsistency, they wilted.

Most of us value consistency over almost everything else.

In the business environment, a seller can profit from our drive to be consistent by getting small commitments from the buyer during the sales process, which lead to a larger yes – *the* yes – in the end. Empirical experiments have even shown that allowing the clients to fill the order (rather than the salesperson), significantly decreases later cancelations and improves satisfaction.

We all strive, consciously or unconsciously, to be consistent and honour our commitments. This is mostly a good trait, but it is important to be aware (as you may find if you are ever arrested), that it 'can and will be used against you'. Most of the times this happens we tend to feel it in our guts. As a counter measure, Cialdini suggests pointing out to the seller that you have identified how your answers are being played against you.

3 Consensus, or social proof

Human beings are social creatures, always looking around to absorb and mimic the accepted behaviours of those around us. We do it from early childhood. It is how we have learned to sit up on the floor, graduate to a chair, and whether we eat using forks, chopsticks, or our hands, depending on what our parents did.

Social proof is the main reason canned laughter was common on TV comedies for so many years. Even though the laughs are fake, they provoke us to conform to the social rule. Companies use social proof like 'most popular' and 'best-selling' to convince us to buy their products. The underlying message is that such an astounding number of people cannot be wrong, so we should conform and purchase.

Brands can also use people we look up to, to encourage consumers to engage. Michael Jackson's endorsement of Pepsi was a huge boost for the brand back in the 1980s. He was a superstar in music, but how did those credentials qualify him to recommend a soft drink? The star-endorsement strategy, weird as it seems, has brought the most unlikely connections between star and product. In recent years we have seen:

- Kim Kardashian & toiler paper
- Robert Downey Jr. & Nissan
- Beyoncé & Toyota
- Taylor Swift & Coca-Cola
- Ozzy Osborne & I Can't Believe It's Not Butter
- Jennifer Anniston & Emirates Airlines
- Justin Timberlake & McDonalds
- Serena Williams & Intel

And lastly, our favourite:

- Gwyneth Paltrow & a psychic vampire repellent spray on Goop.

We all know they will have been handsomely paid. We know that they are not experts in whatever they promote, and we can probably agree they are very unlikely to use many of the products they are shilling for. Does Robert Downey Jr. drive a Nissan LEAF? Does Bey rattle around NYC in a Toyota? Is Serena the go-to for advice on computer chips? Not as far as we can tell. Yet despite its irrationality, star-endorsement clearly works, influencing crowds into opting for certain brands. Humans strive for connection and like to be part of something bigger than themselves. As with all these weapons of influence, social proof can provide a good shortcut to what is appropriate. Though it's important to retain perspective. Know your data, know the market, know your alternatives. Don't let popularity dictate your procurement.

4 Liking

We all agree that we prefer to spend time and work with people we like. What is not always so clear is *why* we like them, and that this preference can be used against us by strangers. We are much more likely to be influenced by someone if we like them too. Salespeople are trained to impress a favourable opinion on their prospects and clients, and that usually means being pleasant and friendly, which is good for all involved. On the other hand, it is also important to separate the product we are buying from the person we are buying it from, because in the end the product is what stays inside our factories or offices.

What then are the ingredients that influence us into liking someone we have just met?

(a) *Similarity:* we tend to like people like us. Salespeople are trained to mimic the body language, speech, vocabulary and gestures of the people with whom they are interacting, to create an artificial impression of similarity.

(b) *Physical attractiveness:* there are multiple studies showing that attractiveness vastly increased a person's chances of being elected for public office (Efran and Patterson, 1976), helps getting hired on a job-interview (Mack and Rainey, 1990), reduces the likelihood of going to jail if you are charged of a crime and will also affect the amount you will likely pay in penalty fines in a court of law (Stewart, 1980). It usually improves a seller's chances as well.

(c) *Compliments:* nobody is as immune to flattery as they think. Human beings like to be recognised and appreciated. When salespeople can communicate compliments to their audiences while remaining sincere, they win points on our unconscious likeability-meter.

(d) *Contact and cooperation:* we prefer what we are familiar with. Many of us will have seen the negotiation tactic where the seller will side with you to battle their boss or headquarters to be able to achieve the right price. It is designed to make you feel like they are on your team. Or they may employ the good cop / bad cop strategy, which can also be a powerful tactic in negotiations.

5 Authority

People tend to defer to those whom they perceive to be credible, knowledgeable experts. Creating this kind of authority can be years in the making. Authority is not just about being right; it's also about being trusted. And trust, like a good investment, increases over time. Just like compounding interest rates, the cost of building authority is always front-loaded. Returns accelerate the longer you stay in the game, but too many people treat gaining authority as a tactical sprint, when it's really an ultramarathon.

Instant credibility is hard to come by. Short-lived fame is often followed by ignominy and regret. People whom we truly admire have often earned their authority over years, even if they look like an overnight success. Do not be blinded by reputation but remember it can matter. Companies have spent years building up their ability to deliver great services as suppliers to customers. Organisations are only as good as what they deliver to customers – their brand perception is their customer experience.

The best suppliers we've met – and the best procurement leaders – are just good at what they do. Most don't win arguments; they don't need to. The authority is obvious for everyone to see.

6 Scarcity

People want more of the things they can have less of. Limited edition cars and numbered prints, one-off pieces of furniture and bespoke jewellery all command a premium. When OnePlus released its first phone, it could only be bought through an invite. The exclusivity and scarcity of these invites made consumers flock and helped it become an established brand. Spotify's launch in the US followed a similar tactic.

It is not enough to explain the features and benefits of your product; you also need to demonstrate their scarcity, and what the customer stands to lose by not buying. If you're a buyer, it's worthwhile thinking about whether this trick is being used on you. A perception of scarcity can make us panic. You only need look at what happened with toilet paper in 2020. It taps into loss aversion and FOMO – documented, powerful forces.

However, scarcity isn't just a sales tactic; you must also assess genuine commercial risk. Real scarcity of supply will hit those hardest who have not planned accordingly. Whether it's market consolidation, a lack of talented resources, sole-sourcing dependencies, or raw material constraints, genuine issues can be impactful if not considered in the planning.

Smart procurement mitigates these potential impacts by using framework agreements, multi-sourcing techniques, succession planning, scenario modelling and contingency planning. Scarcity can help to create urgency – just consider whether it's helping you or your supplier – and it can expose weaknesses in preparation.

Finally...

There are often many, many buyers in a business. Way more individual purchasers than most businesses ever realise. Most of them will never have heard these lessons, and it is human nature to be seduced by some of them. Now that you are aware of these weapons of influence, you have probably realised you have taken the odd shot yourself. You might even have sustained multiple wounds on the same purchase. Maybe now you'll know better how to defend yourself in future. Do not blame the salesperson; show them some respect for being good at their job.

References

Cialdini, R. (1984) *Influence*. Harper Business.

Efran, M.G. and Patterson, E.W.J. (1976) *The Politics of Appearance*. University of Toronto.

Jervis, T. (2025) Thousands of UK drivers share their real-world verdicts on the manufacturers of the cars they own. *Autoexpress*. Available online at https://www.autoexpress.co.uk/best-cars/driver-power/91289/best-car-manufacturers (last accessed 3 December 2025).

Kominek, S. (2020) Porsche reaches top of Consumer Reports' brank rankings; Tesla rises to 11th. *Automotive News*. Available online at https://www.autonews.com/retail/porsche-reaches-top-consumer-reports-brand-rankings-tesla-rises-11th (last accessed 3 December 2025).

Mack, D. and Rainey, D. (1990) Female applicants' grooming and personnel selection. *Journal of Social Behaviour and Personality.*

Shiv, B., Carmon, Z. and Ariely, D. (2005) Placebo effects of marketing actions: consumers may get what they pay for. *Journal of Marketing Research*, Nov.

Stewart, J.E., II (1980) Defendant's attractiveness as a factor in the outcome of trials. *Journal of Applied Social Psychology*, 10.

Wikipedia (2025) Boots theory. Available at: https://en.wikipedia.org/wiki/Boots_theory (last accessed 4 December 2025).

chapter 8

The path to profit

To achieve the best possible value while maintaining fair and sustainable supplier relationships, it is important to follow a solid process.

Whenever a business is looking to make any purchase, there are plenty of widely published processes that can be followed. The numbers of steps and their names vary, but the basis is typically similar. Applying them can work across a myriad of companies, categories, countries and contexts. Standardised processes help to ensure predictable outcomes, reliable performance and a repeatable pattern.

The leading global professional body in the world of procurement is the Chartered Institute of Procurement and Supply, or CIPS, based in the UK (CIPS, 2025). CIPS began life as the Purchasing Officers Association in 1932, and was granted a Royal Charter 60 years later, in 1992. Their work is used as the benchmark in many other regions around the world and provides services for its members in more than 180 countries. Since 2014, it has been able to offer its members Chartered status. We have opted to expand on their process in this chapter.

You can use their step-by-step process, published on their website at www.cips.org to help guide you through your own procurement process. These steps, which form the basis of a best practice procurement process, are outlined in this chapter. Our aim is not to teach you how to run a procurement process; just to give you an overview of the main steps and considerations.

8.1 Define business needs and develop specification

We've already touched on the importance of planning to guard against project failure. The chances are projects will fail at an even higher rate without the correct understanding of the aims and objectives.

As is the case with creating any successful project outcome, we must first define the requirements. Without a clear understanding of the desired outcomes, any poorly defined project is likely to fail. When it comes to a procurement project, especially one aiming to reduce the overall cost, improve efficiency, or both, this is fundamental.

You must know what you want, not vaguely, but specifically. Most businesses and organisations must buy a wide range of goods and services, so it is important to recall *Spend with Purpose*. Whatever you do, it must align with your overall strategy and business goals. Whether you are buying overheads, goods for resale, or vital raw materials for your manufacturing process, myriad options tend to be available, so clear and exacting specifications are necessary. Usually, the tighter that specification can be the better, although there are times when you will need to demonstrate flexibility.

Business needs are often different from department to department, let alone between different companies, so you will need to involve a range of relevant internal stakeholders to help you gain complete clarity of requirements.

8.2 Market analysis and make or buy decision

Once you know what you want, you have a decision to make. In some limited cases, it may be an option for you to make the thing you need. Depending on the context, this could mean physically manufacturing a product or component that answers the business need.

Not everyone is a manufacturer of course, and the 'make' capability is beyond the abilities of most organisations, so more typically, you will need to look externally and identify options in the market. The first thing to determine is the level of your internal knowledge and capabilities to conduct this exercise. You can use the *smarter spending matrix* in the Appendix to assess the strategic contribution of the purchase against its resource efficiency.

Ask yourself:

- Is this purchase important to our business (core / direct or indirect spend)?
- Is it strategically important?
    - You can use the Kraljic matrix to determine the risk vs reward
- How can you administer the costs; is this a capital investment, an outlay, or can the costs be amortised over a period? Are the costs fixed or variable?
- How available is the supply? What risks are attached to it?
- Do we have the internal expertise to truly know all the above, or would we benefit from external resources?

The second step is to determine what sort of market you are entering: is there choice and a truly competitive market to engage with, or are the possibilities more limited? Where there *is* competition, your job is made both easier *and* more complex. Easier, because you don't have the limitations associated with a monopolistic supplier and limited available specifications. More difficult, because you will need to conduct a thorough supplier capability assessment to determine which of the available options is the most appropriate solution for your needs.

Either way, this stage requires research before you make a final decision.

8.3 Develop the strategy and the plan

Once you have a direction of travel, you can decide on your sourcing strategy. Depending on the levels of importance, availability and risk, you will need to decide if you are you looking for a single supplier, or whether you will need several suppliers. You will need to consider the internal landscape too: What will be required to embed the new product or supplier and what resources are available to allocate to evaluation and testing?

You will also need to think about what the other requirements are, beyond the specifications. How does this fit within the wider business strategy, sustainability and social value goals, or the goals related to innovation and growth? Think about how you are planning to run the process of going to market, and what to you need to consider to *Control the Cost of Change*. Who will be required during the onboarding process, how will you approach any governance, or legal questions if necessary, and who will be responsible for the ongoing relationship?

8.4 Pre-procurement market test and engagement

Before you go ahead and do the project, it is sensible to further research the available options. Always remember what you are aiming for. Test the appetite in the market, see what sort of competition is likely, gain some understanding of the pricing and structures and think about how much time is going to be required to get the results you need. *Challenge Assumptions* of what is desirable and affordable.

Make sure you are aware of the risks and continue to engage with the internal stakeholders you identified. They will help you to refine specifications, inform your strategy and feed into ensuring you run the right kind of process. When doing your research, you may wish to speak with other teams or departments and some of the suppliers in the market, in case new, innovative solutions are available, though you should be mindful of fairness and transparency throughout.

The core basis of this step is to have a structured conversation with the market options before committing to the final process, so the process you design and carry through is both executable and designed to provide the optimum outcome. In ideal world, you want the suppliers to want your business – and that means creating appetite.

8.5 Develop documentation RFP and detailed spec

Developing a strong tender document is a vital step of the procurement process. The quality of the document you create can either help or hinder the whole process.

Besides the RFP (Request for Proposal), there are two other tools that may be used, either before, after, or instead of the RFP. They are the RFI and the RFQ. We set out below what distinguishes the three.

- *Request for Information (RFI)* – A preliminary document used when the supply market is less well known. If you are buying new payroll processing software and have little knowledge about what is possible, you may want to send an RFI discussing your status and the challenges you are facing, posing open-ended questions, that leave ample space for the supplier to show its full range of options and fees. In these circumstances, it will usually precede the RFP.

- *Request for Proposal (RFP)* – Contains a lot more details and specification of needs. The purpose is to give the suppliers all the context and details they need to build a proposal, leaving some space for them to be creative and suggest best practices to fulfil our needs.
- *Request for Quotation (RFQ)* – The most detailed document, stating the exact specifications wanted. The supplier has to say if he can fulfil each specification with his standard offer, if customisation is needed or if that item is simply not possible. No space for creativity is left.

For most processes we would recommend an RFP, with a previous RFI if you are not familiar with the market for a complex decision. The RFQ option limits the ability of the suppliers to do something different, and quite often that's precisely where the best ideas come from.

Some companies opt to send out an RFP by email and hope for the best in terms of replies. This method is unlikely to deliver the kinds of results you should seek. Suppliers should be presented with the RFP in a frank and open discussion, either at their place of business (especially in categories that rely on knowing how their operation works) or at yours (as the client).

This approach provides a few advantages.

- The supplier feels more likely to believe they have a chance to win and will therefore invest more time (and margin) in finding a solution that best fulfils your needs.
- A conversation makes it more likely a supplier may suggest alternative products or services that they would not necessarily venture in the writing. Open conversations can lead to a wide range of ideas to explore.
- Meeting the person responsible for your account can give you an impression of the onward relationship should you proceed.

These meetings should be well planned and prepared for. Doing your homework on the supplier shows that you are to be taken seriously. It is surprising how unprepared some buyers and sellers can be for these kinds of meetings. No matter on what side of the table you sit, you should want to be in the position that the other party really wants to work with you.

8.6 Supplier selection to participate in the tender

Before we send the tender out, thought must be put into selecting the suppliers that are to be included in this process. If the previous steps were properly done, some characteristics that qualify or disqualify suppliers may have emerged. Any such limitations should be carefully addressed before they are set in stone.

As an example, if you absolutely need response times of a few hours, you cannot have a supplier on the other side of the globe, or maybe even on the other side of the country. On the other hand, if timing is less of an issue, you may want to consider a wider geographical scope. This enables you to keep your options open until you can weigh their responses against your requirement and budget.

To select which suppliers you should invite, you can investigate them online, through both free and paid databases and websites. You can also try to find which ones are being used by your competitors or by companies in other industries that face similar challenges.

Having the help of an expert at this stage can be quite helpful. As an example, a packaging expert will know which suppliers are the best fit for a certain type of cardboard, whether it can be printed on with graphics, or if the supplier can handle larger or smaller production runs, depending on what you need.

You could decide to only negotiate with your incumbent supplier, if you anticipate the costs of change to be prohibitive. This can happen in certain types of industrial gases, where the supplier owns equipment that could be messy to replace. However, these situations should be the exception, not the rule. Often, the best solutions come from a competitive tender, or at least the illusion of one, motivating the incumbent to sharpen their pencil.

You can also decide not to include the incumbent, or suppliers you have used for this product or service in the past, if you are (or were) not satisfied with their performance. Again, this should be the exception, as the current supplier knows your business better than anyone and is in a good position to offer improvement suggestions.

Throughout, keep in mind that the suppliers know their market way better than you possibly can, so keeping your options open is usually the best strategy.

8.7 Issue tender documents

The invitations should be sent to the suppliers in written format, usually using email or a dedicated software platform.

A clear deadline for the acceptance of proposals should be set. To keep momentum, the date should not be so far ahead as to produce inertia, nor so close as to make the deadline impossible to meet. For some categories, such as electricity or gas, with volatile but simple prices, a few days should be enough, for others, two to four weeks should work. For more complex procedures and specifications, you may need to allow for a process that lasts several months.

The tender document should include required quantities and product or service details and any limitations or special requirements that may exist. If you can, also include as many other details as possible that will help the suppliers to respond accurately. Let them know about typical order sizes, which may be dictated by things like space constraints in the warehouse, as well as any relevant KPIs and Service Level Agreements (SLAs). Where possible, you should also share with them the criteria for selection you will be using as part of your decision-making process.

You can specify the format of the reply and provide an Excel file or PDF for them to fill in, keeping in mind that may constrain their replies and potentially limit the capacity for them to communicate more innovative solutions.

We tend to think it is best to give all suppliers one chance to present their best offer, while making it clear from the start that there will not be second and third rounds of negotiation. This helps to keep the process timeline controlled and avoids the prospect of suppliers holding back their best offer, just in case it is necessary later.

8.8 Bid and tender evaluation and validation

After receiving the proposals, you should compare them thoroughly with your past and forecasted usage (if significantly different). A transportation supplier may present its tariffs offering competitive prices in the first few lines to entice interest, but 'hide' high prices later – showing where they will make their margins. If can review these carefully and accurately against your real consumption, you could realise that the best overall cost may come from what looks at first like a less competitive supplier.

If relevant, consider the total cost of ownership (TCO) when evaluating proposals. The high costs of maintaining equipment may offset its lower price.

Removal and disposal costs may also be relevant in some cases. Before the next step, it can be useful to meet with the top one or two suppliers, to clarify any questions you may have, as well as to see if there is a fit between you and them. When faced with similar offers, choosing whoever inspires more confidence, from either the perceived cultural fit, or even from gut feeling, may be the best solution.

8.9 Contract award and implementation

After the supplier is chosen, a contract may be put in place. If no such formality is needed, or isn't common practice in the industry, it is still best to have some written form or proposal, or even emails, agreeing to whatever conditions you may have, in a way that anyone who may take over the responsibilities or relationship later, can understand.

Appropriate timelines for implementation should be agreed amongst all relevant parties and departments involved in the daily operation. In some areas, for example changing electricity supplier, the implementation must go from zero to 100% in a single moment. Others, for example a new cardboard box or labelling solution, can evolve from small, contained tests, growing up in volume over time, as both your organisation and the supplier feel more at ease by seeing the new relationship work.

In the implementation stage of a new solution or supplier, bear in mind that some time may be needed until it all clicks and the daily operation can proceed without friction. Adjustments from both sides at this stage are often necessary, either to the product itself, the operation, logistics or communication.

Once the contract has been awarded, you should inform the other bidders that they have lost. Provide them helpful information, such as an idea of how much the difference in price was, or on what criteria they fared best and worst. This will both gain you goodwill for future projects, as well as increase the odds that their solutions will be closer to your needs should you need them again.

8.10 Warehouse, logistics and receipt

This heading makes complete sense if you are buying widgets, raw materials, stock or equipment. Under those circumstances, your considerations are things like warehouse processes, space and capacity, storage requirements, inventory management, receiving and quality inspection protocols, and the like.

Where the title itself makes less sense on the face of it, is if you are procuring other things, like marketing or professional services, software or utilities. That does not mean this is a step you can ignore – you just need to recontextualise it. Depending on what we're talking about, think about it more in the sense of 'going live', 'onboarding' or 'implementation'.

For services, you need to think more in terms of knowledge transfer and integration with existing services, systems, or environments. You will still need to consider verification against specifications, possible new training needs with internal staff, go-live support and in some cases, documentation, warranty, insurance considerations and compliance.

8.11 Contract performance and improvement

Once a new supplier or contract has become operational, ensuring it delivers is now your responsibility. Putting in place early, then regular reviews to monitor performance should be built around using meaningful KPIs and service levels that align with the business objectives. Managing contract performance means managing change, and even your best efforts to ensure accurate specifications are still likely to mean that adjustments will be required to optimise the solution and the relationship.

It's not just about measuring and reporting. Quality assurance, feedback from users and stakeholders – including staff and customers where necessary – all form part of making sure the new arrangements deliver against objectives. You are also likely to need to account for the *Cost of Change*, training and new circumstances; things are rarely static.

Keeping a close eye on how things develop, escalating issues back to the supplier where necessary and measuring new costs against historic ones all help to ensure that the new solutions you have selected and embedded work for you in the way you intended.

8.12 Supplier relationship management

SRM is about realising that not all new suppliers, products or services need to be managed and measured in the same way. If you've used the Smarter Spending matrix, the Kraljic matrix, or both – you should have a clear picture of where to focus attention and where to relax more. This segmentation – usually between strategic, tactical and transactional needs – helps you to determine where to apply this effort.

The most effective supplier relationships tend to be those characterised by open communication and genuine collaboration. Good relationships also tend to foster the kind of innovation, transparency, information and risk sharing that drive the best outcomes over time. Recognising good performance and having constructive feedback are the signifiers of a strong relationship – and strong relationships are where improved capabilities and competitive advantage are formed, and this is the object of the exercise.

The best supplier relationships are not those that enforce contractual terms or punish poor performance, but where genuine collaboration can provide benefits for both you and the supplier.

8.13 Asset management

This is another area that most naturally fits in the manufacturing arena that these ideas grew from. Addressing the procurement of physical goods, machinery and parts means tracking things like the condition of the equipment, maintenance and repair, planning warehouse or factory spacing, and eventual disposal or replacement over time. It also includes managing the financial elements, the amortisation of the purchase, insurance, depreciation and the planning of capital investment for replacement.

End-of-life planning includes contingency planning for breakdowns or early replacement and should also consider the ethical, social and environmental considerations of these decisions.

When it comes to reframing asset management for services, the principles remain the same. It just requires a different understanding of what an asset is in that context. It may be things like intellectual property, licenses and terms, knowledge and capabilities, data or contractual rights. You need to consider questions such as:

- What happens when the contract ends?
- What do we own, versus what do we license?
- What happens to our data?
- Have we – and can we – capture knowledge during this service delivery?

Essentially, you need to consider what you acquire – and what you retain – once the contracts come to an end. What are the tangible and intangible outputs that exist beyond the transactional, that require ongoing management, protection and support and, perhaps most importantly, what arrangements are in place to ensure business continuity if relationships falter, contracts expire, or suppliers cease to exist?

Reference

CIPS (2025) The thirteen steps of the procurement process: Use our step-by-step guide to help you through the procurement process. Available at https://www.cips.org/intelligence-hub/procurement/procurement-process#item-block-1 (last accessed 15 December 2025).

chapter 9

Time to rethink

9.1 What is the price of loyalty? Who can you trust?

Many believe long-term relationships are synonymous with good price and service. But loyalty can drift into complacency, where unexamined contracts and uncompetitive pricing become normal. Familiarity dulls discipline, so blend respect with scrutiny.

How would you feel if you found out that the supplier you have trusted for years has been charging you way more than they charge their other customers? Time and time again we find this situation inside our clients. We can recall one law firm client in the UK, who had used the same paper supplier for more than 10 years. Every year they were wined, dined, taken to play golf and provided with Christmas gifts. They should probably not have been as surprised as they were under these circumstances, but we're not ones to judge how angry they became at the revelation that they were paying almost two and a half times the price we subsequently found for them. It powerfully demonstrates the importance of *Building for Visibility* and *Challenging Assumptions*.

Without comparative data, long relationships can mask major inefficiencies. According to researchers from Duke University in the US, this increase in costs the longer the relationship lasts, is exactly what happens to dental customers. They found a very clear relationship: the longer you have been with your dentist, the more money they will charge you (Schwartz *et al.*, 2011). Step forward the American Dental Association (ADA). Of course, they asserted that the industry was extremely professional and expressed doubts about the accuracy of the data in the study. They were, however, unable to provide any evidence to the contrary. One of the authors of this study suggested that dentists are just one of the many service providers where this is likely to happen.

It happens for a good reason: conflict of interest. Any supplier that can keep a long-term relationship with their clients has a huge advantage over all their competitors. Complacency can slip in on both sides. Within the client, two things tend to happen: first, clients tend to settle to a level of satisfaction with the service levels – 'this is how it has always been' – and secondly, fear of change in the client is likely to be high.

This sometimes means the supplier costs, service levels, KPIs and annual price increases are less likely to be micromanaged. They look after the client well, meaning they can charge just a little bit extra for this superior service. The problem is, over the years, as our law firm found out, this 'little bit extra' often compounds into what can became quite significant amounts of money.

The conflict is that on the one hand, in most cases, the supplier genuinely wants to serve the client the best they can, but on the other hand, the motivation for profit is what drives business forward and the motivation for salespeople is commission. In the end, when it comes to long-term supplier relationships, however happy you are, it is likely your supplier is even happier. Reminding ourselves to *Spend with Purpose* means auditing satisfaction by measurement, not sentiment. If your supplier is very cheerful, you might want to wonder where it's costing you.

We do not have a study backed up with data such as the one above to show the standard for B2B relationships. But after many years working in this environment, we can confidently state that the cost of loyalty exists and is often higher than you might think. Another example we recall is from a client who was being served in a certain area by a lifelong friend and neighbour. He told us that much on our very first meeting, and that he was sure he had the best prices and service. Reluctantly at first, he allowed us to analyse the category and work with both his and other suppliers to find solutions that kept quality sky high, and that could also hopefully bring savings and cash for our client.

When we presented the results, the client was in disbelief: all the credible competitors had quoted prices 30% to 40% lower than he was paying. We had to work hard to find excuses for his friend. High prices don't *necessarily* mean that a supplier is automatically invalidated, but it's a useful reminder to measure value and not assume. The friendship was not broken, but the prices went to where they should have been.

We have found many similar stories, often involving even higher percentage savings. For balance, sometimes the opposite does happen: the supplier has forgotten to increase prices quickly when the market has gone up, or has been fearful to do so, and the client has been profiting from amazing conditions. In our experience though, we find one of these situations far, far more rarely than we find the other.

Another extreme case we can recall is that of a supplier of plastic films that every year was being asked by their client to cut down prices by 1 or 2%. Every year, the supplier agreed. At the same time, secretly, they began to deliver less of the material in increasingly large proportions. Over time, the rolls that had originally contained 300 metres of material, now barely contained 200 metres. In the end, when we compared with its competitors for the same volumes, he was overcharging 34%.

As to the question at the beginning of this chapter, how do clients feel when they find they have been overcharged for many years? You will not be surprised to hear that they certainly feel something. Betrayed. Cheated. Hurt. But they should not. Except for that last extreme case we have mentioned, where the supplier was in fact cheating on the amount of material supplied over time, these situations are just a result of human nature and are to be expected. In any case, we would argue that these situations are more often about client behaviour than the supplier.

The seller is acting according to the unwritten rules of the game. Their motivation is clear. Grow the client, increase the amount of business and profits. If they can keep the client happy and loyal then they keep winning. The client on the other hand, feels that anger at least in part at themselves. They have given trust where it was not merited, or not checked when they should have, as they now find out to their cost. None of this happens if we follow sound procurement practices.

We all know this of course, but we tend to think we are better than the rest of the world. We referred to this superiority illusion in Chapter 5. Even now, you are probably reading this and thinking that these situations we describe only happen to other people and not to you. Well, think again, and this time try to assume that you are no better than average and consider the possibilities about what might be. Being better can be achieved in lots of areas, even in most of the areas where you already believe you are on top.

That's why adopting smarter spending principles is more cultural and philosophical than operational. It needs to change mindsets and encourage self-examination. Curiously, as we've seen in the study, the superiority bias also explains the reaction of the ADA. They did not believe it was possibly happening, because they did not believe it could happen to them.

We do not know enough about dentistry to be sure whether we are being overcharged or not. But just in case we are, we have eschewed the tradition of a life-long dentist and now regularly look at who else is available.

9.2 The tyranny of DIY. Lessons from home projects

Trying to do everything in-house can backfire. The hidden costs of time and distraction often outweigh the benefits. Knowing when to bring in outside assistance is a strength that protects focus and accelerates results.

When considering any new home renovation project, we first consider our own skills. Do we have the necessary knowledge, experience and technique to make 'DIY' a viable option in this instance? For something smaller, like painting and decorating, fitting some laminate flooring, replacing a tap, or building an outdoor barbecue, many of us will feel it's within our wheelhouse. However, when it comes to more involved jobs, like landscaping the garden, fitting a new boiler, or rewiring electrics, most of us will default to a professional. The less confident and comfortable we are with a subject – or the more potential for disaster it contains, the more we're likely to realise that our own knowledge has limits.

We already know that our superiority bias means we're more likely to overestimate our own abilities. In these scenarios, we are also likely underestimating the complexity, cost and time taken to do it ourselves. In the same way, business often underestimate the complexity of certain functions, such as software development, networking, or print management. In both cases, failure to recognise the potential difficulty and proceeding without the required expertise can lead to a costly outcome.

That's one of the things *Spending to Strengthen* means, investing in external expertise can build internal capability. Partnering with experts and suppliers is not a sign of weakness, it's a decisive act to transfer knowledge, increase understanding and change culture. As we covered in '*Why you should call an expert*', relying on internal generalists will cap what you are able to achieve, though focus alone should achieve something.

Home projects often drag on, drain resources and end up more expensive than hiring a professional. In business, the same bias means leaders tend to assume that cost optimisation will be a time drain, when really, a well-run project with expert help often takes less than ten hours of client time and delivers some of the best ROI available. So why the reluctance? Too often, cost-saving work is dismissed as a distraction from 'real' business growth. But that's wrong headed. Growth isn't just revenue; it's margin, efficiency and resilience. Ideas that improve spend are ideas that fuel futures.

If your team resists tackling cost, the board should ask 'What story are we telling ourselves?'. Cost reduction is not about trimming pennies. It's about liberating capital. Every pound saved lands directly on the bottom line. That's not just good housekeeping. That's strategic advantage. In the context of business, the decision to keep tasks to an in-house team with limited knowledge, rather than outsourcing to expert partners, can result in missed opportunities for growth and innovation. By focusing on core competencies and outsourcing non-core functions to experts, businesses can unlock new possibilities and gain a competitive edge in the marketplace.

From the perspective of quality control and compliance, there are also tremendous benefits to partnering with the right suppliers or contractors. Any reasonably significant home project may fall short of expectations or even pose safety hazards without professional oversight. The same is true in the office and even more so in the factory, distribution centre or out in the world. Errors in areas such as insurance, cybersecurity and waste management can be costly both in terms of income and reputation. *Visibility* matters, you can't plan to control risks that you haven't planned to see.

Nobody wants to make high-profile mistakes like this at work. But even asking employees to take on responsibility outside of their area of expertise – particularly without training them to do so – can build frustration and disengagement. Businesses that rely on existing personnel and procedures can lack insight and innovation. Collaborating with partners and building new relationships often injects new ideas and energy into companies.

Let us return to TCO: total cost of ownership. When considering all these relationships, particularly with goods suppliers (as opposed to service providers), it's vital to look not at price but at the TCO. Although the upfront costs of DIY will always seem lower, there are also risks and limitations – remember the umbrella? Low up-front cost, high cost-per-use. TCO doesn't lie.

Fitting a new toilet yourself might seem like a bright idea, but it may not feel quite so smart when ankle deep in sewage, calling the emergency plumber. Similarly, in business, you must consider not only the upfront cost but also factors such as the lifetime of the product and the price of any necessary repairs and maintenance. There are also hidden contractual terms and add-ons to consider. In the search for a more circular economy, we must also think about using materials that are fixable, recyclable and easily replaceable.

DIY can be advantageous in the right circumstances, but it is a double-edged sword. Whether it is underestimating time or complexity, neglecting quality control, or a lack of important supply market expertise, the pitfalls of DIY can have far reaching consequences in business, in terms of poor terms on long contracts. Conversely, many businesses are recognising this risk and taking a proactive approach to cost, purchase and supply management, driving innovation, collaboration and sustainable long-term success.

9.3 We still don't have the money

People often feel that improvement is too expensive to even attempt. This thinking locks organisations into stagnation, ignoring the opportunity cost of inaction. Reframe affordability in terms of net benefit and future resilience, rather than just current cash outlay.

Many companies hesitate when they consider starting a cost reduction project because they are afraid of incurring costs during the process. In a sense, the hesitation is legitimate, because most business projects are costly, so the precedent is there to provide succour to that fear. They seldom ask 'What's the cost of not doing it?'. All too often, that becomes an 'unknown, unknown' – and because the outcome is unclear and today is comfortable, all too often, they do nothing. It might feel less like one, but doing nothing is still a decision and, believe us, the cost of doing nothing is almost always higher.

There are two types of costs that stop people from starting a cost reduction process. The first is potential investment and the second is external cost. Let's start with investment. If, for example, you are a manufacturing company, you will know how long your machinery has lasted so far. If your machinery is old, and new equipment will be more productive and reduce the cost of energy or maintenance, investment can look tempting.

Try this:

The following outline allows you to perform a simple cost / benefit analysis, enabling you to decide whether proceeding (or not), is the correct path.

- **Payback Period (PP/DPP)** – the time it would take for the investment to breakeven. The Discounted Payback Period is the same, but considers discounted cash flows, instead of absolute values.
- **Net Present Value (NPV)** – measures the differences between the present value of cash inflows and outflows over time. A positive value indicates a profitable investment.
- **Internal Rate of Return (IRR)** – discount rate that makes NPV equal to zero. Useful when comparing different options.
- **Return On Investment (ROI)** – the percentage return of an investment relative to its cost. A simple way to see the efficiency of an investment.
- **Breakeven** – the point at which total revenues equal total costs.

With these in hand you can make an informed decision about whether the investment is worth it, so long as the assumptions made are reasonable. Looking only at how much it costs is a bad call. Comparing the cost with the results it brings is a much better way to make the decision.

The second cost that delays or stops a cost reduction project in its tracks, is the cost of outside help. Often there is a cost upfront for experts to be involved. If you know how much it costs and how much you can earn, you can use the analysis above to decide. But in many cases, you won't know if the project will generate results. Hiring experts who are paid based solely on results, in a gainsharing agreement, is usually the best solution. In this case, *you can only win*. It allows structured change to be relatively risk free and low impact. There are only two possible outcomes. Either results are achieved and you generate additional profit, or they are not and it has cost you nothing more than a few hours.

You actually do even better than that, because what you also learn is that the aspect of the business you have interrogated is on track and you can focus on others instead – valuable insights that have not cost you a penny. Make sure you align objectives with the experts, so you are both focused on the same outcome: improvement of the bottom line. The goal is not just saving money, but enabling better performance, to generate *Profit fuels Purpose*, fuelling the future. Using a success-fee eliminates the need for calculations: the net return is either zero or positive. You can't lose money on the deal. Cost reduction project too expensive? Bah! Done right, it is *never* expensive.

9.4 We will never use consultants

Some companies enforce a blanket rejection of external advisors, despite reliance on lawyers and accountants. Engaging consultants selectively and purposefully can bring discipline. It is a strategic lever, not an admission of failure.

Marty Kihn, an American writer and former stand-up comedian, popularised a well-known joke in his 2005 memoir *House of Lies* about his time as a consultant. The phrase in question – you've probably heard it before – was 'a consultant is someone who steals your watch to tell you the time'. There are other jokes along similar lines – all designed to poke fun at the 'fact' that consultants charge people an awful lot of money to tell them something they already know.

Obviously, we're going to say this, but equally obviously, it's simply not true. Deloitte, PWC, KPMG and EY cannot be some of the most well regarded and profitable firms in the world without delivering value to their clients. After all, they are pretty expensive. Thinking with *Value before Cost*, these firms and Accenture, BCG, McKinsey and the rest wouldn't keep getting paid if the investment in them didn't drive real commercial gains, making their fees not an expense, but an investment.

McKinsey has produced more leaders of the world's largest companies than anyone else. This is not a coincidence: these firms provide an excellent grounding for business professionals to succeed. Although R&D does not guarantee success, and despite these origin stories, Alphabet still spent $55.63 billion dollars on it in the year to September 2025 and Amazon's spend had grown to a whopping $102.69 billion in the same year (Macrotrends, n.d.(a) and (b)).

The other accusation levelled at these major players is that they charge substantial money for a report, then leave the implementation to the client. This can be true to some extent, though not all consultancies – and not all consultants – are the same. For many companies, however, the 'we don't use consultants' mantra becomes lore, though this rule is rarely written in stone. Or to put it another way once more, it is simply not true. You can bracket their partners and advisors as 'lawyers', or 'tax specialists' or 'auditors', but semantics aside, they are using external consultants on a regular basis – even those that say they have a policy that prevents them from doing so.

Organisations of all shapes and sizes use these external experts to provide specialist knowledge, information or resources as part of their day-to-day. Whether tax, legal disputes, HR, or import / export advice. This applies to independent business owners working as just one or two people in the businesses all the way to FTSE 100 companies, so it certainly applies to every SME in between. As well as this generalised feeling that consultants are there to take your money and tell you what you already know – sometimes rebranded as 'validating your existing thinking' there are also usually one or more of three issues behind this statement.

- **Comfort** – everyone prefers to work within their comfortable zone, even if the magic tends to happen when we get outside it. It's only human. We've come across so many cases over the years where we've uncovered outrageous and unethical price rises caused by cosy relationships that become warped in favour of the supplier over a long period.

- **Trust** – in a similarly comfortable scenario, people need to trust whoever may be helping them. This can lead to a situation where you may only trust those suppliers with whom you are already familiar, creating a 'closed shop', with little room for improvement or innovation.
- **Bad past experiences** – if you have previously worked with a consultant and it has gone poorly, it's understandable that you may be reticent to do it again. On the other hand, you have probably had a bad experience at a restaurant, but it hasn't stopped you eating out. It is important and *fair* to recognise the tax adviser that saved you from a bigger bill, the employment lawyer who prevented you from being sued into oblivion and the insurance broker who made sure your losses were covered after the flood. Think about it properly and that one poor experience of professional services is probably the exception, not the rule.

Hiring consultants in and of itself is neither good nor bad. The results you generate by working together can be either of these outcomes. From our experience, agreeing to share the risk and rewards provides the best outcomes. Even the biggest consulting firm charging models are changing, with clients demanding they take on board more risk. This reflects a growing awareness that smart businesses must *Control the Cost of Change*, by structuring support in ways that protects them from downside and focuses everyone on outcomes.

9.5 Costs are dealt with overseas

Centralised procurement can sometimes create a sense of helplessness locally. But treating group-level decisions as reasons for disengagement is a mistake. Even in global structures local teams can create value by gathering data and escalating.

'We're not allowed to touch that' should be what sets off the klaxon here. Not because you want to meddle, but because it should warn you that it could mean 'nobody is really looking at it'. Let's use the UK for this example, but it could be anywhere. Let's say you are a UK subsidiary of a business headquartered in Sweden. You look at the P&L, and it shows you that half of your large budget lines – for IT, Facilities Management, Managed Print, Marketing Print and Telecoms – are all locked into group level contracts.

What's the reaction? Impotence. *'We're not allowed to touch that'.*

Fast-forward 12 months, your business has dipped slightly, all the contracts renew at higher prices and suddenly, you are being told to cut other costs – worst of all perhaps personnel – to make budget.

For some of our readers, this will sound familiar. 'Overseas' is a mindset as much as it is a geography. 'Overseas' is a shrug of the shoulders, or a collective sigh. It's absolving yourself of responsibility and placing it somewhere 'other'. Does that sound like best practice? Just because something is centralised, doesn't mean it's optimised. Contracts negotiated by global headquarters can be slow, bloated and generic, compared to the localisation and agility that would be desirable. It's easy to trust the mothership – until you realise you are the ones it's going to cost.

Local teams hesitate to get involved in scenarios like this because they fear overstepping and being shut down. They can lack access to data that could give them a more credible challenge, and worry that in any case, the gains might not be big enough to bother rocking the boat for. We know of one gym chain who were locked into a low-speed Wi-Fi agreement with a HQ contract. Despite finding a better solution locally with improved tech and faster speeds for a third of the cost and an option to give notice built into the contract – they were blocked from doing so, because it broke protocol. The result was membership attrition and increased costs. Hardly ideal.

When spend is treated like this, however, it disempowers local initiative and innovation, which we can all agree is a bad thing. Local teams see waste others don't, but staying quiet is not going to improve much. Over time, that silence can aggregate into substantial unnecessary profit leakage. One trainer tells a story that demonstrates perfectly how people are risk averse when it comes to gains, but risk-seeking when it comes to losses. Tell someone their water bill is higher than it should be, and the response is often 'Whatever, I've got bigger fish to fry.'

Take them out into the car park and show them water gushing out of a leak just after it's passed their water meter and you can be sure someone will be on the phone to the supplier within the next 10 minutes. Demonstrating visually how much you can be bleeding cost is a wake-up call. This is where *See the Whole System* meets *Challenge Assumptions* – and where *Build for Visibility* becomes the difference between oversight and outcome. The bigger picture here is that the business should be doing what is best, not what is easiest. Lazy assumptions like global beats local pricing were dealt with back in Chapter 5.

Just because you are told costs are dealt with elsewhere, doesn't mean you should stop asking questions. 'That's just the way it is' doesn't need to be forever, and just because you've got *a* solution doesn't mean it is optimal. *Good Enough* isn't a strategic approach. 'Costs are dealt with overseas' isn't a strategy. It's a habit. And bad habits cost money. If your local entity is carrying the weight of someone else's decision, speak up. Silence isn't loyalty. It's leakage.

References

Kihn, M. (2005) *House of Lies: How Management Consultants Steal Your Watch and Then Tell You the Time*. Hachette Book Group.

Macrotrends (n.d.(a)) Alphabet Research and Development Expenses 2011-2025 | GOOGL. Available at https://www.macrotrends.net/stocks/charts/GOOGL/alphabet/research-development-expenses (last accessed 12 December 2025).

Macrotrends (n.d.(b)) Available at https://www.macrotrends.net/stocks/charts/AMZN/amazon/research-development-expenses (last accessed 12 December 2025).

Schwartz, J., Luce, M.F. and Ariely, D. (2011, Nov) Are consumers too trusting? The effects of relationships with expert advisers. *Journal of Marketing Research*, 48 (SPL).

Statista (2025) Annual revenue growth of management consultancies worldwide from 2015 to 2024. Available at https://www.statista.com/statistics/936889/management-consultancies-worldwide-annual-revenue-growth/ (last accessed 4 December 2025).

chapter 10

Supplier relations

10.1 Terms and Conditions: Having fair supplier terms is not soft – it's strategic

Many costly disputes start with poor contracts. Treat Terms and Conditions as strategic tools rather than administrative afterthoughts. Clarity and foresight in agreements can prevent confusion, protect value and strengthen relationships.

In the ultimatum game experiment, one player has the power to split $10 however they like with another; to walk away with the money both must agree (Guth, 1982) . If the offer is too low – even a free dollar – most people reject it outright. Fairness, it turns out, matters more than free money. Most of us would rather walk away with nothing than accept a deal when we know someone else took too big a share of the cake. 'Enjoy your $10', we think, 'I hope it buys you some manners'.

Part of the purpose of this book is to ensure you are never in a situation where you fear – but don't know – that this might be happening to you. Salespeople may have to sell to anyone willing, just to pay their bills, but they prefer to deal with buyers that treat them fairly. Creating a strong working relationship can make for reciprocity, where a fair deal for all sides is achieved. This is of course the ideal world. As a buyer, you can't just expect reciprocity to exist on the other side. You'll need some checks and balances.

Optimising costs almost always involves a large measure of optimising supplier relationships. In a B2B environment, these will mostly still be with people you can talk to and reason with. As such, it is vital to establish good working relationships with these other companies. Some buyers still treat suppliers as subordinates, not partners. This strategy may work at times, but it rarely pays off in the long term. It has many disadvantages that become clear when the relationship is continuous, or the product or service has a bit more complexity (as most do).

One is that the person on the other side will have little incentive (other than getting the money in) to provide you with the best solution. Humans are emotional. If they feel poorly treated there is a good chance they will actively dislike you. They may still provide what you've asked for but will abstain from suggesting the best solution or going the extra mile. And because they know their market better than you do, it's likely that if anyone's losing out as a result, it's you.

Smarter supplier relationships

Imagine a company has two clients facing temporary cash-flow problems. One has built a great relationship with the supplier, calls to explain the problem and offers a payment plan. The other has treated the supplier like dirt and just stops payments without engaging. Who will continue to get supplied?

Building a relationship based on fairness and reciprocity is almost always the best path. The exceptions, besides the one-off simple transaction, are when dealing with sharks – they will feed on whatever you offer or push for more. Fortunately, sharks are not that common in most B2B sectors. Bringing fairness to the forefront of B2B deals is also important because it allows the discussion to be broadened, from price only to the many other important factors that are valuable. These may be:

1. **Operational flexibility:**
   - *Speed of delivery* – you may get a better price if you are willing to accept longer delivery dates.
   - *Warehousing* – the supplier may agree to store goods for you if you agree to buy them in the next few weeks or months.
   - *Production planning* – if you can provide estimated purchases for the next 6 months or year, it will make the supplier's job easier and bring you advantage.

2. **Financial levers:**
   - *Payment terms* – be aware that longer payment terms will probably mean a higher price.
   - *Rebates* – for meeting certain purchase thresholds.
   - *Insurance or liability coverage* – for the inevitable rainy days.

3 Quality and Support:

- *Quality* – in some specific product areas you may be willing to accept sub-standard quality, at a discount.
- *Warranty* – you may need longer terms than usual, or you might even want to dispense with them altogether.
- *Post-sale support* – you may want to agree conditions at an early stage.
- *Bonuses and penalties* – some conditions may be so important to you that you may want to include penalties in case certain measured goals are not achieved.
  - In that case, it may be fair to include also provisions to pay a bonus to the supplier if they surpass their goals. For example: penalise the supplier if service levels fall below 95%, but reward them with a bonus if they achieve 97%. *Our grandparents would call this the carrot and stick method.*

4 Exclusivity and compliance:

- *Packaging or labelling needs* – you may need more or less of these than what's standard for the supplier to provide.
- *Restrictions on selling to competitors* – these may be possible, but the cost may be steep.
- *Length of the agreement* – the longer the contract, the better the conditions should be.
- *Mitigation strategies* – for supply chain disruptions.

This list is by no means inclusive of all the conditions that are valuable and should be included in the conversation with the suppliers. On the other hand, it may be best not to overwhelm the suppliers at an early stage. Only the real deal-breakers should be talked about when asking for a quote. The best proposals can then be discussed and the more complex solutions worked on together, in a collaborative spirit.

Throughout the process, keep in mind that some of these terms and conditions are more valuable for you than the supplier, and vice versa. The importance and value of each will differ in each case. The ideal would be to concede on the ones less valuable for you and get the supplier to concede the ones more valuable on your side. Bend enough to keep the relationship stable, but never enough to break either party.

It's interesting to note that there are a couple of curious footnotes in the ultimatum game.

Firstly, most people – between 60% and 80% – split the money evenly. Treating others fairly is not only in our best interest, but also the most human path and the one that will make us sleep better at the end of the day (Kahneman, 1986).

Secondly, when the money increases from $10 to $100, the number of rejections of unequal splits increases massively. The more money at stake, the more fragile the relationship becomes – and the more important it is to ensure both sides feel respected and rewarded.

10.2 How many suppliers should you have?

Too many suppliers dilute leverage and add complexity, while too few create dependency. The right number is specific to context, and leaders should be deliberate rather than defaulting to either of these extremes.

We often hear procurement teams and other budget holders asking. 'What is the ideal number of suppliers?'. It's a fair question, but it's also the wrong one. At least without the supplementary '*for what purpose*'? The good news is that we can answer that dilemma quickly. The bad news is we've been here before. Once more, the answer is 'it depends'.

There are many advantages to having few suppliers, or in extreme cases, just one. Greater volume provides greater negotiating power, lower administrative costs (fewer invoices to process, and fewer payments to make), greater quality control, reduced complexity and fewer stakeholders when problems arise. If the relationship is well managed, it can even create the kind of proximity that creates innovations that can benefit both supplier and customer.

On the other hand, the disadvantages of the single supplier model are also clear. The biggest is the supply risk. If we depend on a single supplier and they fail, not having an alternative can be painful. The lack of competitiveness can also cause higher prices. In our experience, the comfort of a single-sourcing relationship often leads to the supplier discreetly increasing prices over time, especially for new or unusual products, or they abuse the trust placed in them by maintaining prices while cutting back on other variables that time has taught them are not being measured by you – remember the 200-metre long 300-metre roll?

If single sourcing brings clear advantages and risks, it's no surprise those of multi-sourcing are opposites: better competition and resilience, but increased admin and looser relationships. Returning to the initial question, what is the most appropriate number of suppliers in each cost category? The answer 'it depends' can be based on the following variables:

- *How critical the process is* – if it is critical to the company's activity, then having more than one supplier is desirable. You can't rely on a single point of failure.
- *Ease of replacement* – in some areas, qualified suppliers are abundant and can be quickly replaced. In this case, having only one may not be a problem.
- *Volume* – spreading a low level of purchases across many suppliers can cause us to be insignificant to all of them, meaning we never get access to the best conditions. On the other hand, if the volume is large for the market, dispersion can allow for good conditions by putting pressure on competitiveness.
- *Size of our organisation* – according to a 2018 Forbes report, multinational *TotalEnergies* has more than 150,000 suppliers; a small company would not be able to manage this volume, or anything close to it. In general, the larger the company, the more suppliers it will be able to manage efficiently.

Try this:

To decide on the right number of suppliers, query these five key factors:

- **Criticality of the process:** is it business critical or easily replaceable?
- **Ease of substitution:** how hard is it to switch?
- **Volume of spend:** can we command leverage, or are we spread too thin?
- **Organisational scale:** do we have the infrastructure to manage complexity?
- **Innovation & complacency:** are we being too loyal for too long?

You can repurpose the smarter spending diagnostic tool you'll find in the Appendix to score these out of 10 and plot the answers. The larger the area covered – the higher the score in each area, the more suppliers are needed to spread risk.

To give some concrete examples, let's consider electricity. There are excellent suppliers in this area, but as it is a commodity, they are easily replaceable. Having a single supplier for several facilities simplifies processes and gives access to better conditions than having several different suppliers at different sites. Express transport and some common plastics could be other examples of this case, where the disadvantages of having more suppliers far outweigh the advantages.

On the other hand, for a product that is critical to the functioning of our organisation, it makes sense to have more than one alternative, as the risk is extreme: it could paralyse the company. For most cost categories, it makes sense to have between two and four suppliers, allocating larger shares of our purchases to those with the best quality / price ratio, ensuring a balance between the advantages and disadvantages of extreme models. Even more important than the number of suppliers we work with is ensuring that they are the best for our profile. There is no point in having the most appropriate strategy in terms of numbers if the suppliers are not the most suitable for our organisation and aligned with our mission.

In any long-term relationship, there is a mutual adaptation, which gives incumbent suppliers a great advantage over others, as time will have smoothed out any rough edges in the service. On the other hand, time tends to create complacency. We become accustomed to levels of service that may be far from ideal. It is important for the organisation to remain open to new suppliers who can bring innovation and new practices. To send this signal to the market, you should periodically consult alternative suppliers, not to validate what you already think you know (our suppliers and solutions are the best), but with real openness and the intent and agility to change whenever it is rational to do so.

In an increasingly complex world, the answer 'it depends', while frustrating, is a good one. It forces us to think about the relevant factors and find solutions that work best, although it is only useful if it leads you to better thinking. The ideal number of suppliers is the one that balances risk, leverage and readiness to adapt. Only by placing these questions in your own context can you decide that, so try the exercise.

10.3 Competitive positioning in supplier interaction

Understanding suppliers' pressures and incentives creates more productive outcomes. Buying excellence is built deliberately through effective research and preparation, not by chance or luck.

Often when we consider a sales interaction, we picture the salesperson showcasing their wares to the client, and the client making the call on whether to proceed. In our experience though, it is also always in the clients' best interests to position themselves well to the seller. Don't just evaluate suppliers; become an attractive partner that's worth working with. Each supplier will have their favourite customers. And human nature means favourite customers are likely to get access to pricing and incentives not available to regular accounts.

Any client who fits the criteria for 'ideal' tends to enjoy better conditions, whether on price, quality, or service. It is up to the buyer to position themselves and their company as ideal clients. Of course this begs the question: What makes an ideal client? The answer depends on the sector, the timing and the market conditions, but there some characteristics that suppliers tend to look for.

- Buys in large volumes
- Pays promptly
- Well known – so can serve as a testimonial to other prospects in the sector
- Well organised – they order well ahead of needs, avoiding urgency
- Simple to serve – no trucks waiting too long to unload or rare technicalities
- Geographical location – close to the supplier or its mains routes
- Loyal – does not change supplier often
- Courteous to deal with
- Allows comfortable margins

As a client, we should wish to embody most of these traits. However, we do not wish to become the *perfect* customer. 'Perfect' would mean never questioning pricing, never switching suppliers and paying a premium without realising it. Remember, all businesses exist to make profit margins, and this includes your suppliers. All kinds of businesses will have their favourite customers, and what they usually mean is the ones that pay the most. The trick is to be an ideal customer in every way but that.

We still want the things that are important to our company: better prices, longer payment terms or a special service level. Inherently, there is a problem here. Favourite customers tend to pay well, but good customers also want good pricing. This is why we need to consider the process of selling ourselves to the customer, by positioning our company as a client very close to that ideal.

We may know that we're unable to (for example) meet the quantities of other customers. However, we can use other characteristics to position ourselves in a way that becomes attractive to any supplier tendering for our business. To do this most effectively we need to position our company in a way that leverages our interests.

For that purpose, we should do our homework before we even reach the supplier, preparing answers to questions like:

- Where are they located?
- Where are their main clients?
- What sector or niche industries do they mostly work with?
- Who are their main competitors?
- What are the most pressing challenges of their industry?

It is also important to hear the suppliers and understand what they specifically value most in a client, and what their own characteristics and challenges are. If we can, it is better to understand this correctly at various levels (the company, its directors, the salesperson), since the person you are dealing with may have different objectives to the overall business.

You may have heard the phrase 'think of a number and double it' when trying to estimate a complex cost. In some industries, sellers assume that when a prospect talks about volumes, they should quote on half only, as they are used to companies overstating their minimum volumes, then subsequently ordering far less, hoping to take advantage of volume pricing. It seems like it could work as a one-off trick, but the reality is ineffective in the medium, or long-term, as suppliers will understand and adapt. Worst, they will mistrust whatever else the client tells them in the future.

Far better, for the relationship and for accuracy's sake, to simply be transparent in the first place. For instance, 'last year we have bought 194,232 units, 5% below the previous year. This year we plan to recover and are estimating a requirement of over 210,000 units'. If seasonality is relevant in your world, then share the historical monthly averages with the supplier to demonstrate the likely requirements each month. It will help them to adjust their process to your needs, as well as giving credibility to the projections.

Throughout the purchase process it is important to maintain trust. In the same way we want to retain trust in our suppliers, so too should we also keep our promises, enabling them to trust us in return. If we can build new relationships with potential partners based upon mutual trust, we can feel confident that the door remains open in future, if we are unable to reach an agreement to proceed immediately.

The methods we describe demand more effort from purchasing teams than the approach we tend to see in SMEs, which is often that approach of pitting three similar suppliers against each other and hoping that the best conditions result from the process. Our process involves more work, more time and more dedication, all of which are scarce resources. But guess what? Taking this approach will lead to better results, better conditions and better, more sustainable long-term relationships.

10.4 Market variations and how to approach them

Many companies must buy supplies where prices are linked to fluctuating global markets. Analyse spending strategically to understand where each should be applied for maximum benefit.

Many products bought by companies are directly or indirectly linked to fluctuations in local, or global markets. Commodities like oil, energy, metals, paper and plastics are usually quoted in markets, or else price variations are accompanied by industry indices. Sometimes, suppliers and manufacturers take advantage of these variations and use them to generate a substantial margin. It is therefore important to keep an eye on how the market is changing, so that we are not the ones being taken advantage of.

This is where it is important to *See the Whole System*; understanding not just our suppliers, but the markets and forces that shape their thinking and their prices. But can we – and should we – try to forecast and anticipate trends? We believe the answer can be found in the Chinese story of Sai Weng that goes like this:

'Sāi Wēng lived on the border, and he raised horses for a living. One day, he lost one of his prized horses. After hearing of the misfortune, his neighbour felt sorry for him and came to comfort him. But Sāi Wēng simply asked, 'How can we know it is not a good thing for me?'

After a while, the lost horse returned and with another beautiful horse, a mare. The neighbour came over again and congratulated Sāi Wēng on his good fortune. But Sāi Wēng simply asked, 'How can we know it is not a bad thing for me?'

One day, his son went out for a ride with the new horse. He was violently thrown from the horse and broke his leg. The neighbours once again expressed their condolences to Sāi Wēng, but Sāi Wēng simply said, 'How can we know it is not a good thing for me?'

A year later, the emperor's army arrived at the village to recruit all able-bodied men to fight in the war. Because of his injury, Sāi Wēng's son could not go off to war, and was spared from certain death.

In business too, the wisest attitude is to be like the Sāi Wēng: wait and see what the future brings, because trying to predict the market is a fool's errand. The same logic that underpins the smarter spending matrix applies here: focus on where you can make the most impact. You cannot control all market movements, but you can elect to focus on what matters most. Start with two dimensions: how critical it is to your business and its relative cost to you. Plotting this gives you clear visibility of where price volatility carries risk.

Once you see that picture, you focus your efforts on where both value and vulnerability are highest – the equivalent of the 'refine' and 'repurpose' zones in the matrix. These categories are where strategic actions make the biggest difference. For items that are neither costly nor critical, standard contracts or index pricing may be sufficient. For those that are volatile and / or critical, more advanced tools may be needed. These could include fixed-price agreements, dual sourcing, or hedging instruments that help you to *Control the Cost of Change*, even when you can't predict it.

Markets will always move. The aim of the game is not to predict in which direction, but to build a procurement strategy flexible enough to deal with lurching in either.

10.5 Negotiation in practice

Successful negotiation relies on effective preparation, empathy, courage and timing. We show that clarity of goals and willingness to walk away from the wrong conditions are the foundation of effective negotiation.

Anyone who has children or a partner, recognises the fact that negotiation is a fact of life. The art of ending up in agreement can sometimes be achieved easily, or it *can* lead to a tantrum. And not just for children.

Yet in most western cultures, when you go shopping, the price is the price – except in the US, where tourists are often surprised by the taxes added at the register. What something costs has fluidity, but our regular shopping trips trick us into thinking prices are fixed. It takes a bit of discipline and intentionality to *Challenge Assumptions* where familiar purchases are concerned, but those that do it discover there is often more flexibility and value than they thought.

Here's another question with a fluid answer. *How much is your house worth?*

Last time, did it sell for the asking price? Last time you *bought* a house, did you pay it? Negotiations are a part of our daily lives. Negotiations are also a part of our global culture, whether the Good Friday agreement in Northern Ireland, the war in Ukraine, or the conflicts in the Middle East, negotiation has enormous power and great responsibility.

Yet in business, negotiation is a space that doesn't command too much attention. Perhaps because it is away from the glamour of the sales pitch and the vital detailed planning and analysis of the finance team. The work tends to happen quietly, in the background. Subtly, every day in conversations, in emails. These interactions are rarely high stakes, often nuanced and tend to be unglamorous and unrewarded.

They can, however, indicate the profitability and health of a typical business or organisation. How disciplined are staff? How cost-conscious, or how wasteful is the culture? These are important questions, because overhead costs don't make money, they take it. How much they take, how much you are prepared to let them take, is up to you. You can't operate without these costs, but you can make leaner, smarter decisions and leave more room for financial flexibility, growth and resilience.

Negotiation – an overview

When it comes to negotiating in business, there are plenty of very good books written on the topic already. The aim of this chapter is simply to give you a condensed understanding of negotiation as it relates to buying for your business.

Negotiation is about two or more parties reaching agreement. There are only a couple of ways in which to approach it. Competitive negotiation requires a winner and a loser. A collaborative negotiation aims for win / win.

Both require an understanding of context. If you are buying a trinket from a garage sale, or a second-hand piece of furniture from a place you will likely never visit again, you will probably drive towards a competitive negotiation aiming to win. This way, you get the best possible price and leave nothing on the table. Even if you leave the other person feeling like they've lost, there is no ongoing relationship to concern you.

On the other hand, if you are dealing with a supplier with whom there will be an ongoing relationship, a win / win solution is more desirable. The first method works for people who do not know one another, and do not care. In purchasing for a business, the second scenario is most commonly the right strategy, so we will focus on that, although most of these techniques can be used in both cases.

Think about how much an hour of your time is worth. Whether negotiating in your private sphere (for a new car or house), or for a single large purchases or small repeat business for your company, a few minutes of negotiation can generate *a lot* of money. Learning how to do it well is one of the best investments of time you can make.

Step 0 – Preparation

The most important step in any negotiation is before it begins. Preparation. Most negotiations are won or lost at this stage. This is a core application of *Building for Visibility*. Preparation gives you confidence and leverage. It's the flashlight that reveals where real value resides – and how to claim it. If the other side has not prepared as well, or at all, you start with a huge advantage.

You cannot talk about negotiation without referencing the art of war. The Chinese General Sun Tzu put it clearly 2,500 years ago:

> *'If you know the enemy and know yourself, you need not fear the result of a hundred battles. If you know yourself but not the enemy, for every victory gained you will also suffer a defeat. If you know neither the enemy nor yourself, you will succumb in every battle.'*

Ideally, you should avoid a negotiation altogether and just get what you want. You don't walk into an Apple or Tesla store and discuss price or terms and conditions. There are no special sales or bulk discounts. They just set the rules, and you either accept them, or you don't.

Before going into a negotiation, you should be able to have a reasonable idea of what the main goals and objections from the other side are likely to be and be clear on your own. You should prepare replies and counterarguments for these. Don't focus too hard on the difficulties, but don't avoid them. Focus on putting their objections to the forefront of the discussion, but from your perspective.

Using your perspective is important, and you should always use it to underline your strengths. If you are a small company, do not articulate it by implying the spend will be small, emphasise instead that you will be an easy organisation to work with.

Most negotiations boil down to the weakest argument losing. That's why preparation is so important. When preparing your case, you should use multiple layers. If you are clear on your objectives and truly *Spending with Purpose*, you know what matters to you, and can build toward the desired outcome.

This reminds us of an Aesop's fable. Near death, an old man gathers his warring sons together. He binds together a bundle of sticks and asks his sons to break the bundle. They cannot. He unbinds the bundle and demonstrates how easily individual sticks can break. This object lesson in unity also applies to the unity of purpose in gathering your arguments for a negotiation.

You must have multiple layers, but do not include too many, or your argument will be reduced to its weakest one. Anyone sharp will focus on your one position that does not stand up to scrutiny, so you lose, even when you have plenty of other valid points, As you will also know, trying to defend that point is a waste of time; your counterpart will ensure the discussion turns on your weakest argument and you lose.

When building your case, also plan for your points to tug at their emotions. It is easy to focus on the facts and the numbers, forgetting that the other side will likely decide based on emotions and then justify to themselves afterwards with reason. Collaborative negotiations are important, because if the other side doesn't like you or doesn't feel appreciated, they are unlikely to offer the best conditions or will feel justified in imposing future margin increases or extra service charges.

A concept that is essential to have prepared when going into any negotiation is your BATNA (best alternative to a negotiated agreement). You don't *have* to close this deal. There are usually other suppliers, products or services that will do instead. Defining the parameters – the highest price, lowest payment terms or minimum delivery standards that are acceptable is essential.

Going back to the Sun Tzu quote, knowing the other side's BATNA is also important, though more difficult to ascertain. Understanding their industry and its trends will help. Talking to competitors or colleagues of your counterpart will also contribute to a better understanding of the full picture. During the negotiations, the other side may let slip some information, although this should be greeted with some suspicion. Try to spot potential concessions or trade-offs that may be more valuable for them than they are to you.

Another important point to prepare is the *anchoring*. It is hotly debated if making the first offer is better or worse. If the supplier sets the price, they will never know if the buyer was prepared to pay more. On the other hand, they may set a price so high that they price themselves out of a deal there and then. The advantage the seller has in making the first offer is that it anchors in a value and provides a starting point for discussion.

In another study from 2003, subjects were asked to write their last two digits of their social security number and then asked if they would pay that amount for a bottle of wine. They were then asked how much they would pay for other items (chocolates, books and computer equipment). The students who had the highest social security numbers (80 to 99) bid highest, while the reverse happened with the ones with the lowest numbers (01 to 20).

The effect wasn't minor; it was huge: the bids from the 80–99 group were between 216% and 346% higher than those from the 01–20 group. This demonstrates what the sellers already know – price is fluid, and some prospects will pay a lot more than others.

In a market where the ballpark of prices is well known, these differences will be smaller. As we've mentioned, we can tend to think of ourselves as different to the people in the study and that this effect only happens to others. Still, even if it only happens to others, why not use it? The people you are negotiating with are 'other' after all.

If you are on the buying side, you can say something like:

'Well, I'm not expecting to pay just a dollar for it…'.

Importantly, this phrase doesn't commit you to anything (you are saying you *won't* do it), but it does put a very low number out there, into the mind of the other side.

In his book *Pre-suasion*, Robert Cialdini gives the example of a consultant that proposed projects of around $80,000 to his clients. He always faced resistance to his cost, until he started adding the following to his pitch.

'I will not charge you a million dollars for this, it's only 80,000 bucks'.

It may *seem* very simple, but it does work often enough.

In many negotiations one side has more bargaining power than the other, and this is often (but not always) the buyer; they can take their business elsewhere. Sometimes, the supplier has the upper hand. There are situations where there may not be much in the way of real alternatives to a given supplier. In difficult locations or very niche markets, there may not be many, or even sometimes, any choices. Even in this situation though, the buyer can turn things to their advantage; remember, your apparent position of power is meaningless if you don't use it.

Ultimately, they don't know what cards you hold, and you don't know what is in their hands. Being well prepared and presenting yourself in the best possible light make it possible to bluff your way into appearing to have more power than you do, which brings us neatly to step one.

Step 1 – Approach

Your approach should reflect your preparation, so you should be confident and relaxed.

How much confidence you approach the negotiations with can influence how successful you are likely to be. If you can remain relaxed and confident throughout you will listen better, and listening to the other side is vital for success. During exchanges in conversation, it is important to remember a few things. All too often, we can make the mistake of using the time the other side is talking to prepare to jump in with what we want to say next. Instead, we should listen mindfully to what they are really saying.

There will be clues in there as to how far they are willing to be flexible in this area or that. Normally, you should speak less than the other side too. You should be comfortable with silence, and it should have the effect of making them comfortable too.

After all, in many cases although you are building a potentially long-term relationship, you should not fall into the trap of conceding too much ground just to please. Establishing rapport between the two sides helps create common ground and makes it more likely a mutually beneficial arrangement can be agreed.

Step 2 – Clarification and honesty

A communication standard really, but especially important in a negotiation setting. Think about an argument with a toddler. Saying they can have a biscuit later is meaningless to them. Saying they can have a homemade chocolate chip cookie after dinner is specific.

Be specific with your demands when preparing. Be clear that deliveries are required by 8 a.m., or that you need someone on call for maintenance or legal advice 24/7. You do not want to find out too late that your assumptions were incorrect. It is important each side is clear with the other and that there is nothing left to chance. If things are, wrong interpretations and regrets are likely on one side or the other in future and that's not the basis for a happy relationship.

It is therefore important to ask questions to zero in on the details. Is the other side posing a legitimate question, stating an objection, bargaining, or using an excuse to exit? If you are not clear, ask them. Remember, you can ask whatever you want – even difficult questions – if you ask in the right way and defuse the tension whilst doing so.

It is also a good idea to be authentic and express your feelings. The good thing about telling someone how you feel across the table in a negotiation is that whatever you tell them you feel, it is essentially non-arguable. If you say 'I feel disappointed because…' no one can argue the fact that you feel that way. It does also contribute to the other side perceiving you as more authentic and trustworthy. Finally, it also encourages their own capacity to embrace their emotions, which can also work to your advantage.

Step 3 – Understand 'why'

Motivation is key. Imagine two people walking along a river when an orange drops from a tree above them. They both catch it together and argue bitterly about who gets to keep it. In the end, they agree to split it in half. One goes home, squeezes his half orange, drinks the juice and throws away the peel. The other goes home, zests the orange peel, bakes a fragrant cake and throws away the segments. I think we can all agree that could have worked out better.

In this area, it is key to understand the difference between your opponent's *interest* and their position. Their position is determined by their statements and their willingness to give in certain regards. Their interest though is why they want it, or why they want it 'that way'. In that simple example, both wanted the orange, but for different reasons. Sometimes, you and your interlocutors' 'why' is different, but still entirely compatible. You could both have all the bits of the orange you need.

What can you work out about the other person's why? Are they trying to impress their boss? Or are they fearful of their reaction? Can you tell the difference? Try to find out and there may be some concessions you can make that are of little or no consequence to you, but valuable for the other side and count as wins for them.

During a negotiation you want as much as you can to persuade the other side that they've won, while winning yourself. As we said you want to be the ideal customer in every way except paying them high prices. It's the epitome of *Value before Cost*: recognising that true value includes long-term trust, reputation and continuity, not just a low price.

Familiarise yourself with the weapons of influence that you read about in Section 10.5. These persuasion tactics are powerful tools in negotiation, but only if you recognise when they're being used on you.

Step 4 – Use or identify power gambits

During the late 1970s, a few years after founding the Virgin brand, but not so far in that he was yet very wealthy, someone introduced Richard Branson to the British Virgin Islands.

Branson, who was becoming famous, made his interest known and a real estate agent offered to take him on a visit, which he accepted on the proviso that he could take his girlfriend with him. After being flown around Necker Island by helicopter, Branson was told the asking price. Six million dollars. By now, they had fallen in love – him and his girlfriend with each other – and them both with the island.

He made an offer, which was as much as he could afford at the time of $100,000. The realtor considered the offer so derisory that Branson was asked to leave the hotel they had booked them into and make his own way home to London. A year later, Branson was informed that the owner's circumstances were becoming more urgent, and that he was now desperate to sell.

By now, Virgin's business had grown, so Branson was able to afford more. He incrementally improved his offer and the owner – who had never visited the island – eventually agreed to sell to him for $180,000.

Branson managed to buy Necker Island. Not for a minor, or even a major discount, but for a mere fraction – just 3% – of the original asking price. An astonishing result. The kind of deal most of us would never believe was even possible and would never have tried. It has been his home ever since.

It's a great story and an incredible deal, but breaking it down, there are tangible reasons as to why and how he managed it. He was persistent. He discovered the owner had never even been there and needed the money to buy a house in London. Branson asked for far more than he expected to get. He anchored a very low value against the high asking price. He also knew the seller's current conditions and needs and used them to close the deal.

These are just some of the tried and tested methods negotiators can use to improve their position. We would always advocate using such methods in an ethical manner. Of course, understanding these tactics means that you can also recognise them and respond appropriately when they are used on you.

Here are some of the most powerful techniques:

- **Ask for more than you expect to get** – you need to start higher (or lower) than you think, and sometimes at an artificially high level.
- **Silence** can be a great ally in negotiations, embrace it, don't fear it. In tense moments, make it a game in your mind: who talks first loses.
- **Reacting, instead of responding:** one simple way to gain some advantage is to immediately flinch at a proposal: 'Oh no, that is way too much!'.
  - Another is to say: 'I know you can do better than that'.
    - In both cases, stay *silent* after you utter these phrases, no matter how long it takes.
- **Confrontation:** try to avoid it where possible but do not fear it. Often, disagreements can damage the ability of each side to find rapport, leading to poor outcomes. Sometimes though, confrontation is inevitable. Still, the best outcomes come when both parties feel they have something they perceive as a gain, so confrontation is best defused if possible.
- **The trade-off:** Whenever you are about to concede something, always ask for a trade-off: 'I can agree to that, if you agree to extend payment terms to 45 days'.
- **Good cop/bad cop** – we've all seen the movies where one of the cops is intimidating, so that his partner can then act as a friend of the suspect and get him to confess. In negotiations this tactic is also used quite commonly. If you are on the other side of this one, defuse it with humour by calling it out: *'are you using good cop/bad cop on me?'*.
- **Other stakeholder management:** It strengthens your position to have someone from outside the table that approves the deal, ideally a committee. Even the President of the United States needs to revert to the Senate. *'I'll have to get the Board's approval on this'*. To prevent the other side from using this trick, try *'If this proposal meets all your needs, is there any reason why you wouldn't give me a decision today?'*. If they still insist on the Board try asking to meet them or else say *'they always follow your recommendations, don't they?'*.
- **Bluffs** – just as in a poker game, you can either bluff or be bluffed into believing the other hand has a better hand than they do in fact have. The better you know their market, the harder it is for them to bluff.
- **Intimidation** – one side can use intimidation tactics. We don't advise that you are the one to do it, as it breeds ill-will. If they use it on you, however, you have our permission to use it back. Or you can smile and suspend or cancel the negotiation.

- **Time constraints** can be used against you if you let them. Let's say you need to close the deal before you must leave for the airport. Knowing that, the other side can go slow and then offer their final terms just before the taxi is due. Decisions made under duress are not usually the best. There is always tomorrow.
- **Offer withdrawing** can be a powerful gambit, to be used only in extreme conditions. It is normally accompanied with the higher authority excuse ('I'm sorry but the Board has just said we cannot keep the conditions I had offered.'). If they use it against you, evaluate if it may be a bluff. If so, call it. If not, re-start, knowing your position onwards will be frail.
- **Closing.** Just before the close of the process, the other side can ask for one more detail that benefits them. Do not accept it. Instead of accepting, reopen the negotiation and ask for trade-offs.
- **When meeting halfway isn't.** It's common to split the difference and for that to be acceptable to both sides. Let's simplify and focus on a simple price negotiation where the seller asks for 150 and you offer 130. Wait. Let them make the first move. Meeting in the middle and agreeing 140 seems straightforward, but if you let them move first and then invoke your committee / approval process, you have already moved the goalposts. Now, your position is unchanged at 130, but they have now already said they are happy to meet at 140. Next time you go back and let them know your committee would not agree, the midway break point is now 135. They've come down 15 and you must only go up 5. Congratulations, you've almost succeeded in your negotiations!

Step 5 – Close

Before closing, make sure that all details are set and agreed upon. Don't assume they are. Reflect and feedback all terms and conditions. You may not have the opportunity to do it again and things can turn sour fast if one side assumed one thing and the other the opposite. Closing well therefore also demonstrates the benefit of *Controlling the Cost* of *Change*; clarity now prevents hidden cost and unexpected problems later. What seems like an unbelievable success looks a lot more believable when it has been broken down. After all, you eat an elephant one bite at a time.

Perhaps the best advice we can give you about how to behave during a negotiation is simple. A man walks into a bar and notices a dog playing poker against humans. He spots the owner and says to him 'Is that your dog? He's *incredible* at poker!' 'He's not really', the man replies, 'Every time he gets a good hand he wags his tail.'

During a negotiation, never be the dog that wags your tail. Signal nothing, expect everything and leave the room with more than you walked in with. Some proclaim that in negotiations you should 'not get emotional'. We disagree, as we humans are emotional creatures, so that would be denying our nature. Recognise the human in you and in the other side and use that to your advantage. Good procurement makes complex feel seamless. Great negotiation makes essential needs feel invisible. When everything is done right, the only thing anyone notices is that everything just works – affordably, reliably, sustainably.

References

Ariely, D., Loewenstein, G. and Prelec, D. (2003) Coherent arbitrariness: stable demand curves without stable preferences. *The Quarterly Journal of Economics*, 118 (1), 73–106. https://doi.org/10.1162/00335530360535153

Cialdini, R. (2016) *Pre-Suasion: A Revolutionary Way to Influence and Persuade*. Random House Business Books.

Güth, W., Rolf Schmittberger, R. and Bernd Schwarze. B. (1982) An experimental analysis of ultimatum bargaining. *Journal of Economic Behavior & Organization*, 3 (4).

Kahneman, D., Knetsch, J.L. and Thaler, R.H. (1986) Fairness and the assumption of economics. *Journal of Business*, 59, 285–300.

chapter 11

What happens next?

11.1 What do you do in a volatile environment?

Economic forecasters warn that volatility will define the next decade. The organisations that thrive will be those that act decisively, with clarity and purpose. It is unwise to delay decisions, waiting for a certainty that may not arrive in time.

We live in turbulent times. Deep crises are followed by painful but relatively quick recoveries, and when the economy appears to be reaching cruising speed, the clouds of uncertainty thicken again. Companies live with daily risks and many opportunities. Which are the most pressing? Let's look at some of the risks that companies may be exposed to.

- *Politicians:* trade wars and extremist governments are items that appear on the news daily. The effects can be enormous and trigger new global crises.
- *Tax:* all governments like to tinker with taxation.
- *Technology:* it disrupts sectors and eliminates even well-established companies. Remember Nokia, Kodak or Blockbuster? Could your sector be next? They didn't think so either. Nobody is immune to disruption.
- *Markets:* transport, fuel and energy are some of the costs that rise frequently. Salary increases, new legislation, CO_2 licenses and the common ups and downs of supply and demand all move the marketplace in unforeseen directions.

Regardless of the causes (which are of limited interest given that most companies can do nothing to change them), it seems certain that some costs will have significant increases and that revenues may not be as expected, since they are exposed to a global market full of uncertainties.

Contrary to what it may seem, we are optimistic. We have daily contact with excellent companies that, in addition to risks, see plenty of opportunities. These are the organisations that *Spend with Purpose*, who don't wait for certainty to act but instead align their decisions for long-term value and resilience.

Even knowing that the basis of our sample is companies that want to continually improve (which is also why they hire us), it seems clear that there are openings for all.

- *Global markets:* the world is vast and there are still some blue oceans, although it can be increasingly difficult and expensive to find them. A trade war closes some markets but may make others more accessible. For example, a currency devaluation in another country can also make the raw materials we buy from there cheaper.
- *Technology:* is both a risk and an opportunity. Netflix is much bigger than Blockbuster ever was. New technology can reach where old technology could not. A healthy treasury allows you to invest in innovation, buy a promising startup, or imitate its models (lean startup practices, for example, are being implemented by non-tech giants). Allocating capital to build what the business can become is *Spending to Strengthen* in action.
- *Knowledge and creativity:* the adoption of new solutions can completely eradicate some costs. For example: there is no electricity cheaper than that which is not consumed, and different packaging systems may require smaller quantities for the same level of protection of the products.

The companies that thrive will not be the biggest or even the boldest, but those that make decisions with clarity, intention and discipline. Those that hesitate will likely fail. Decide who you want to be, before it's too late.

11.2 Sustainability is survival

Environmental stewardship is an existential imperative, not a PR exercise. Reducing waste, reusing resources and building circular models are all paths to long-term resilience. Sustainability is not optional – it is a strategy for survival.

Maybe the problems start in the consumer world, perhaps at the supermarket particularly. We are conditioned to believe that environmentally friendly is more expensive. Why? Organic milk and organic chicken are more expensive than their regular alternatives, and therefore everyone seems to assume that more sustainable equals more expensive.

However, we should flip that on its head. You've probably heard the mantra 'reduce, reuse, recycle' that we referenced earlier. These three words also represent a radical reframing of growth: *Enough is a Strategy.* These words should also lead you to believe that things can be cheaper too. After all, if you reduce usage, less material is required; that's cheaper. If you re-use something you've already got, it is cheaper than buying a new one. And recycling materials is typically cheaper than digging it up.

In the context we are framing this within, the United Nations introduced the concept of 'Environmental, Social and Governance' at their conference in 2005. ESG investing principles were designed to guide businesses towards prioritising environmental and social issues alongside corporate governance – going beyond Milton Friedman's mindset. It widened businesses' remit in that as well as selling their own products or services, they also assumed responsibility for doing so in a way that provides a net – or net zero – contribution to the wider world and community.

Corporations now bear a greater responsibility for ensuring that their business is 'sustainable'. But what does that mean? After all sustainable simply means continuous and viable. We all want that for our businesses.

For sustainability in this context, let's look at 'Earth Overshoot' day. The day is defined by think tank 'The Global Footprint Network' as the date on which each year, individual countries used up all their annual allocation of natural resources. Top of the league, using up a year's worth by 11 February, comes Qatar. In second place is Luxembourg. Third is the UAE who've used it all up by 4 March, fourth is the USA on 14 March and trailing in shamefully alongside them on 15 March is Canada in fifth place. Pedro's Portugal has used everything up by 28 May, with Neil's UK using it all up by 3 June.

The only countries even getting close to only using a year's worth of resources in a year are Ecuador, Indonesia, Iraq and Jamaica, who all use a year's worth of resources by November. Nobody even makes it to December. Humans currently use up as much biological resource each year as if we have 1.7 planet earths. Given that we only have one, we can agree that continuing like this meets the definition of 'not sustainable'.

According to the WWFs Living Planet report (WWF, 2022), since 1970, the planet has lost 73% from the sizes of our wildlife populations. Again, these numbers point to an *unsustainable* decline. They are true in every region of the world across all major categories, mammals, fish, reptiles, birds and amphibians. The primary reason for this astonishing decline – in every region – is habitat loss due in large part to the human food system.

The WWF closed its report by warning that the world is fast approaching irreversible tipping points that could negatively impact the environment, human society and the future of your children. This isn't just an environmental concern, it's an imperative to *See the Whole System*: society, nature, business and the long arc of human wellbeing.

As well as the dwindling number of harvests able to be supported by our degrading topsoil, we will have to deal with the impact of climate change on migration. Between 2008 and 2016 the average number of people displaced globally by climate change was 21.5 million, which rose to 32.6 million in 2022 (IDMC, 2016).

According to international think tank The Institute for Economics & Peace, this figure is set to surge to *1.2 billion* people by 2050 (McAllister, 2024). Consider our usually imperfect responses to mass immigration and you may give yourself permission to think there might be problems coming. Rising seas, floods, storms, wildfires, droughts and other natural disasters could displace record numbers of people, bringing with it the associated issues over resources.

With all those seemingly terminal problems being recognised as approaching fast, you'll no doubt be pleased to know that humanity has had lots of meetings about doing something about it. In Geneva, in 1979 came the First World Climate Conference aimed at discussing human caused climate change, sponsored by the World Meteorological Organization. By 1988, they and the UN had also created the oft-quoted Intergovernmental Panel on Climate Change (IPCC) – they of the now famous 'hockey stick' graph we became familiar with through the work of Al Gore.

The first COP summit took place in 1995 and the Kyoto protocol, designed in 1997, then came into effect to reduce greenhouse gases in 2005, although without a signature from the world's largest economy in (at the time) the US. Late as it was, the 2015 Paris Agreement, aimed at keeping world temperature increases below 2° and pursuing 1.5°, served as a sign that further progress was being made.

Also in 2015, the UN member states signed up to a list of 17 sustainable development goals to meet by 2030. Though with a wider remit than only the environment, these goals were set up to reduce inequality, restore social justice and raise living standards. Alongside Climate Action and Responsible Consumption, were areas like No Poverty, No Hunger, Good Health, Quality Education, Gender Equality and Clean Water and Sanitation, all designed to help redress the balance in a challenging world.

If you thought the meetings of these august institutions must mean we are doing something right, you would be wrong. 2024 was the hottest year ever recorded. As 2023 was before it and 2022 was before that. You can bet your bottom dollar the trend will continue. Despite 29 COPs and another 16 COP Biodiversity conferences, we continue to warm our atmosphere each year. Since the first climate conference, the volume of CO_2 in the atmosphere and the global temperature have both reached record levels. Since Greta Thunberg's school strike, since all of it, things have only got worse.

I guess all of this is our subtle way of saying that we need to do more. Much, much more. At its most basic level, the definition for sustainability is simply the ability for something to continue. People regularly get confronted with all kinds of phrases around sustainability. 'Global warming' and 'climate change' – even 'climate crisis' but let's not forget the planet was here billions of years before we were, and all the evidence points to it being here long after we are gone. This is not a crisis for the planet; it is a crisis for *humanity*.

Sustainability is not about preparing for a change in the weather: you might think it hysterical, but we're talking about the future of the human species' ability to inhabit the planet. Not in a nebulous timeline, in a comparatively tangible one. We need to think and behave radically differently.

It's therefore time – well past time in our opinion – to put more sustainable thinking at the heart of everything we do. We believe all our principles can help us to do that. Time to place long-term survival and equity at the centre of decision-making. To make that work for you, follow the themes we define below in whatever the best way you can apply them.

Sustainable procurement – our definition

Sustainable procurement is the process of purchasing goods and services in a way that delivers long-term value not only to the business, but to society and the environment. It involves considering the full life cycle impact of what is bought. From extraction and manufacturing to transport, usage and disposal, and making decisions that reflect the organisation's wider responsibilities and goals.

It is not simply about selecting greener products or complying with regulations. It means *Challenging Assumptions* about cost, quality and speed, so you can ask better questions: What is truly needed? What will reduce waste? What improves resilience, equity and efficiency over time?

At its core, sustainable procurement embeds three key shifts:

- from short-term to long-term value
- from siloed choices to systemic thinking
- from reactive compliance to proactive design.

It aligns with the smarter spending principle that *Sustainability is Survival*, not a cost. When you reduce usage, you save money and resources; when you reuse or refurbish, you extend life and lower waste; and when you source responsibly, you complete the circle, giving resources a second life.

Sustainable procurement is how organisations – and nations – can lead on climate, fairness and transparency through the very act of spending. It's a practical tool for influencing markets, improving social outcomes and future-proofing operations, all while basking in the glow of doing what's right. If sustainability is survival, then procurement becomes your plan A. There is no plan B, unless governments and societies also adopt our principles.

11.3 Artificial intelligence – this time it's different

> *AI is new, but here to stay. Automation, prediction and generative tools will reshape procurement and operations. Experimentation now is essential to avoid being left behind later. Embracing AI with clear purpose is a competitive necessity.*

With the advent of large language models (LLMs) such as OpenAI's ChatGPT, Anthropic's Claude, Google's Gemini, or Microsoft's Co-Pilot and others, it is hard to find your way through a newspaper or magazine, without stumbling upon several articles about artificial intelligence or AI. Indeed, it's difficult to look at an image, or even a video now, without questioning the reality of what you are seeing. What was that about technology reaching a point where it is no longer distinguishable from reality and living in a simulation?

Let's move on. A preponderance of these articles seems fixated on one topic. Is AI the greatest opportunity mankind has ever created, or its greatest threat? In all honesty, most spend more time on the catastrophic than the idyllic. But we've been here before. Another reason *Challenging Assumptions* resonates is that we tend to go overboard for novelty. Or dismiss it too soon. Which is probably not sensible in this case.

We don't always remember, but we've been told many times before new technology will be the end of us. From the Luddites anti-machinery riots to the advent of the printing press, and from 3D TV to Google Glass, these things have either not been the end of us or haven't taken off at all. We have been hearing about the imminent breakthrough in virtual reality since the early 90s. Despite

Meta, owner of Facebook and Instagram investing billions in it, there remain few signs of a breakthrough.

By 2018, it was Blockchain that would revolutionise supply chain management. Seven years later there is not much happening. Success stories in a business environment are few and far between. Whilst the technology is a fantastic solution, it feels like one still looking for the problem to solve. So, should the title of this chapter be: 'Artificial intelligence: *is it* different this time?'

Artificial intelligence itself has been a recurring theme every 10 or 20 years. After *Metropolis*, it was *2001: A Space Odyssey* or *Blade Runner* that provided unsettling visions of the near future and technology running unfettered. The '*Terminator*' series and the '*Matrix*' trilogy repeated the recipe with enormous success.

Futurists like James Lovelock, Ray Kurzweil and Matt Ridley all refer to 'The singularity', an idea first developed by IJ Good, a British mathematician who worked at Bletchley Park with Alan Turing. In his 'intelligence explosion' model from 1965 he posited that an AI agent could enter a feedback loop of such constant, accelerating improvement, that this 'explosion' in intelligence would create a superintelligence that would surpass humanity. The singularity refers to the moment that happens.

In his book published in 1999, Matt Ridley describes this moment as inevitable, estimating that this moment will happen in less than 100 years. For Kurzweil, in his 2005 book, the prediction was for 2045.

The biggest companies in the world are investing many billions in the inevitability of this technology immediately, but that still doesn't guarantee anything. Microsoft lost out on the smartphone market by electing not to invest, instead believing that desktops – Bill Gates' dream of a computer in every home – was still the right call. They can get this stuff wrong.

Which reminds us of a Monty Python sketch, in which a man sees sheep voluntarily throwing themselves out of trees trying to fly. He asks the shepherd what is happening and why he is letting it continue when they don't so much fly, as plummet to the ground. 'Because of the enormous commercial possibilities should they succeed' says the shepherd.

Technological companies cannot afford to fall behind their competitors. Even if they don't know the answers, they are forced to invest by market imperatives. On the other hand, they could be convinced and later proven wrong.

There is also the question of time. Omnipotent or even conscious AI may be inevitable, but how long's it going to take? Some goals that seem just around the corner persist in escaping: we have no flying cars, no lunar bases and frustratingly, still no hoverboards 40 years after we first 'heard the name McFly in the

1985 film *Back to the Future*. Even fully autonomous cars have been teased as being here 'next year' for at least 10 years (let down by Elon Musk *again*).

Putting the cynicism to one side though, the LLM's we've seen really have improved substantially and the leap from watching an awful, hilarious AI video of Will Smith eating spaghetti from a few years ago, to what we've seen recently from tech like Veo3 is genuinely scary. There's plenty of belief that this time AI is here to stay, that, this time, it really will be different.

AI business success stories already abound, from customer service contact centres to its use in investigations, whether by journalists, medics or the police. We now have much better automated translations, images and sounds, and it has also improved areas like credit assessment, fraud detection and many more.

For example, in logistics, AI is being used to in complex supply chains to optimise delivery routes, as well as predict demand. In the production area, to optimise tasks, inspect and improve the quality of products or predict equipment failures.

On the other hand, AI can even serve to bring viability to some of the technologies that until now have been more promises than certainties. In a world where everything can be falsified with AI, Blockchain technologies could serve to guarantee the veracity of content. VR powered by AI will be more powerful, and may finally be able to fulfil that long-delayed promise.

If progress in this area is great in the coming years, as seems likely, the biggest opportunity and, simultaneously, the biggest challenge for individuals and organisations will be how to best incorporate AI into their lives. Creativity, vision and speed will be even more important qualities. Now is the time to *Spend to Strengthen* our capabilities and capacity, investing in the education, skills and tools that support adaptability and innovation.

The overwhelming majority of companies do not have the billions of an Apple, Microsoft or Alphabet to invest in solutions from scratch. They can trust that the solutions those companies develop will reach the market, but they will still have to adapt them to their reality. More than that, organisations of all sizes will have to be very attentive to practical cases in their industry and in different ones. AI can optimise sales, marketing, costs and processes. Ignoring it could be fatal. Some investment will be essential, and even if at this stage it is 'just' time rather than money. Now is the moment to get a feel for the *Cost of Change*.

Experimenting at low cost now can avoid catching up expensively later. Do your best to understand it. Or hire someone that does. History gives us some reassurance that it is not always necessary to be the first to develop a solution. Being a pioneer has high costs and a low probability of success. Being the second, more creative person to apply or sell solutions can be worth it. Remember how the Wright brothers stood on the shoulders of giants. Apple was not the first to develop the digital music player.

At the speed we are running, 'waiting and seeing' will be too late. 'Learn and wait' may be the best recipe for most companies at this time. In a world of uncertainty, we must play with the probabilities. Like sustainability in the earlier section, AI is another systemic challenge with high uncertainty. However unlikely it seems that computers will be our master soon, we still say please and thank you to LLMs. After all, when it comes time to welcome our new overlords, manners have cost nothing. If you learned nothing else in this chapter, take that advice! But this chapter cannot conclude without linking AI to sustainability. AI data centres lap up huge resources, and nobody wants Al to choose between drinking water for humans and cooling their server rooms.

11.4 The buying olympus

Procurement has evolved from a transactional role to a strategic enabler. Respecting and involving procurement early is what unlocks potential to drive innovation and manage risk. Collaboration and visibility transform buying from cost control into value creation.

A young man asked Socrates if he could ever reach Olympus, that is, become a god. The wise man replied: 'As long as you make sure that every step you take is in that direction'. Someone that followed this advice was Milo of Croton, a six-time Ancient Olympic wrestling champion, who remained unbeaten for more than 20 years.

As a child, Milo had asked Pythagoras for advice about how to become the strongest man in the world. The master told him that he should walk a hundred steps every day, carrying the same calf. Over the years the animal gained weight and Milo's incremental strength increased until the fully grown Milo could carry the fully grown bull. Day by day, step by step, he became the man he wanted to be.

The role of procurement has become more strategic in recent decades, step-by-step. Two of the causes for this greater importance reinforce each other: globalisation and competition. In increasingly global markets, and in lots of areas, strong competitors can emerge from virtually anywhere on the globe. This means that companies must expand the geographic area in which they search for suppliers to vital areas of their business, or their competitors may get ahead of them, significantly reduce costs and take market share. The enormous specialisation and complexity of supply chains also contribute to the strengthening of the role of those responsible.

Another factor that makes the role of supply chain even more vital is the growing importance of sustainability. In recent years, we have seen crises, pandemics, wars, inflation, blockages of one type or another of both the Panama and Suez canals and subsequent breakdowns in supply chains. Suddenly companies were faced with multiple problems.

The scare was enough to shake them. They realised that resilience in the supply chain was not a luxury. If they didn't pay more attention now, the next disruption could be enough to break them.

Increased focus on supply chain is the perfect intersection of the principle that *Sustainability is Survival*: short-term cost is often the price of long-term success. Many years ago, a salesman told us that when he went to one of his clients to announce a price increase of 2 or 3%, the Purchasing Director left the room and came back with a belt. 'I'm at the last hole,' he told him, 'I have nowhere else to go.'

The perception of procurement is changing. Businesses increasingly foster a culture that everyone is important and with greater understanding of interdependency and better communication it's becoming increasingly clear to everyone that without good purchasing, good sales can never be made.

A purchasing department needs to be valued to be valuable. *Spending with Purpose* means recognising procurement not as a service function, but as a strategic enabler of outcomes. There is little point in one that orders what other departments tell it to. Collaboration is key and there are experienced specialist buyers out there who can provide simple, money-saving advice at renewal time.

For a marketing department, the exact size of the label on a bottle, or the exact dimensions of a flyer on a print run may seem of paramount importance, but if the buyers knows the printing industry standards, and knows that by taking a millimetre off the width you can save the supplier a bucketload of grief and yourself 20%, you can at least try to persuade marketing not to waste the money. Stranger things have happened.

In precision engineering and specialist manufacturing, procurement can add substantial value. There's no point a design team spending months on specification whilst holding the mistaken assumption that the materials they plan to use are on budget, when market changes mean they are way outside. Or that they can use a particular piece of technology or materials that are currently experiencing delays in delivery.

Respect buyers. Let them *See the Whole System*. Bring them into the process early and eliminate waste. Let them get to know the process in depth and involve them in the decisions. Procurement can contribute to specifications for more efficient solutions, and this is where the big gains are usually hidden. Skilled buyers add value far beyond price negotiations. Investment in them is *Spending to Strengthen*, making it vital that you give procurement a seat and an active voice at the decision-making table.

In many organisations this elevated importance has led to a rebranding of the department itself, with many changing from 'Buying' or 'Purchasing' to 'Procurement' or 'Supply Chain'. We do see CEOs spend more of their time with suppliers, although probably not as much as they should, and certainly not as much time as they spend with customers. We also see that more leaders have passed through acquisition departments in recent years, before being appointed to manage large companies. In the last ten years, the CEOs of General Motors, Coca-Cola, Walmart and of course Tim Cook at Apple, all began their careers in this department. What was once an almost dead archive of professionals can today serve as a launch pad for the highest positions in the biggest companies.

A Chinese proverb says that 'a journey of a thousand miles begins with one small step'. In the last 10 or 20 years, many steps have been taken towards a more strategic vision for integrated company cost management. Many others are yet to be taken. Is step-by-step is how we climb to Mount Olympus? Maybe it's not completely out of reach.

References

Internal Displacement Monitoring Centre (2016) Global report on internal displacement. IDMC. Available at https://www.internal-displacement.org/globalreport2016/ (last accessed 9 December 2025).

Kurzweil, R. (2005) *The Singularity Is Near: When Humans Transcend Biology.* Penguin Books / Duckworth.

McAllister, S. (2024) There could be 1.2 billion climate refugees by 2050. Here's what you need to know. Available at https://www.zurich.com/media/magazine/2022/there-could-be-1-2-billion-climate-refugees-by-2050-here-s-what-you-need-to-know (last accessed 9 December 2025).

Ridley, M. (1999) *Genome: The Autobiography of a Species in 23 Chapters*. Fourth Estate, UK.

WWF (2022) Living Planet Report 2024. Available at https://livingplanet.panda.org/en-GB/ (last accessed 12 December 2025).

chapter 12

Put smarter spending into action

12.1 Renewed focus

> *Hidden costs are like leaks below the waterline: silent, steady and eventually catastrophic. Spending is both a mirror and a lever: it can identify misalignment and enable improvement. Smarter spending is a statement of intent.*

Many of the costs we discuss – overheads, indirect costs, Goods Not for Resale (GNFR) – don't shout; they whisper. They operate quietly, often out of direct sight, accumulating slowly and steadily. This subtle accumulation can place increasing strain on your margins, your team's time and even your organisational equilibrium. A leak that eventually jeopardises your vessel.

Relying on inadequate tools to examine these costs or drawing incomplete insights from available data can ultimately lead to your demise, mirroring the fate of President Garfield. Cost is not just to be accepted, nor is it just an expense to be minimised. It is a revealing lens, a powerful lever and a critical language. Throughout this book, you have encountered stories that illustrate how unoptimised spending isn't merely inefficient; it can lead to overlooked vulnerabilities.

It can create holes below the waterline, leaving your organisation susceptible to unexpected challenges. Smarter spending, conversely, is not just about effectiveness; it is a clear expression of organisational resolve and strategic intent. It is the conscious choice to build a robust operation that not only stays resilient but navigates with clear purpose and enhanced capability.

We've discussed rising above conventional thinking, the hidden costs of inefficient processes, the importance of employing the right analytical approaches and escaping the limitations of rigid budgeting. Our aim has been to provide you with a refreshed perspective, a new lens through which you can perceive your organisation's financial dynamics with greater clarity. We anticipate that, once you engage with the possibilities afforded by this renewed focus, you will begin to see opportunities that were previously obscured.

You have the potential to initiate significant positive change within your sphere of influence. Leadership positions confer the ability to review and refine processes, streamline bureaucracy and evolve organisational culture away from outdated systems of thinking. The stories and metaphors shared throughout these pages were designed to illuminate fundamental truths, revealing how cost can serve as a dynamic signal; a guide that points to inefficiencies, misalignments or significant untapped opportunities. Smarter spending isn't just a message; it's a mandate. Now it's over to you.

12.2 These principles in action – the power of integrated thinking

Wherever you look in the business world, you can observe these ten principles actively shaping successful financial management. They are not isolated directives but components of a powerful, interconnected framework, forming a comprehensive approach to spending that, once truly understood, reveals significant layers of potential.

Spend with purpose

Your spending should be a direct reflection of your core organisational strategy and values. Continuously ask, 'Does this expenditure truly embody our mission and intent?'. The disciplined approach seen in organisations like Apple, where every product and initiative aligns precisely with their strategic blueprint, demonstrates how purposeful spending minimises misdirection of resources. This principle is fundamental; without it, even robust financial controls can inadvertently support activities that drift from the organisation's true direction.

See the whole system

A significant portion of organisational inefficiencies often occur where responsibilities or information flows are fragmented. A narrow perspective can inadvertently create substantial costs, even when individual departmental efforts appear optimised, simply because the overall system is misaligned. Recalling the parable of the blind men and the elephant (look it up!), it's crucial to perceive beyond individual components. Comprehensive insight into your spending truly emerges from understanding the full context of interdependencies, revealing the hidden costs and latent opportunities that reside in the connections between processes and departments. This holistic view is often complex to construct, yet essential for effective intervention.

Challenge assumptions

We propose that unquestioned historical logic can be one of your most significant and subtle overheads. It is remarkably easy to limit future potential by adhering to yesterday's thinking. Continuing to operate solely on past precedents may only yield familiar, and potentially suboptimal, outcomes. The willingness to scrutinise ingrained practices and long-standing agreements is what uncovers innovative and more effective solutions, often revealing significant savings and new avenues for value that were previously dismissed as impossible.

Value before cost

A low initial price tag is not always indicative of true value. Depending on the nature of the expenditure, genuine value typically emerges from factors like the achieved outcome, long-term durability, effective risk reduction, or enhanced organisational morale and capability. As seasoned professionals in capital expenditure often confirm, prioritising the lowest initial cost can paradoxically lead to greater overall expense down the line. Avoiding the allure of false economy means meticulously evaluating each investment not merely by its price, but by its lasting strategic impact and comprehensive return.

Profit fuels progress

Sustainable profits are vital for funding your organisation's future growth and providing stability for your business and its people. When approached strategically, profit is not an end, but a powerful enabler. It is the fuel for intentional reinvestment – into innovation, into sustainability initiatives and into strengthening core capabilities. Organisations that actively channel profits back into their core purpose, like Dyson's commitment to R&D, demonstrate how financial success can directly empower strategic advancement and continuous evolution.

Sustainability is survival

Inefficiency is a form of waste, and conscious consumption and circular practices encourage a culture of thrift. Beyond simple cost reduction, integrating sustainability into your spending decisions can unlock tangible financial benefits and enhance reputation. The demonstrable value generated by initiatives like Marks & Spencer's Plan A highlights how environmentally and socially responsible practices can lead to significant operational efficiencies and bolster brand equity, providing a compelling return on a foresight-driven approach.

Control the cost of change

Change is an inherent and unavoidable aspect of any dynamic enterprise. However, its financial and operational impact is profoundly influenced by the decisions made in anticipation and during its execution. Inadequate scope control, for instance, can lead to substantial organisational inefficiencies and unforeseen expenditures. The disciplined approach to mission objectives and accountability exemplified during the space race provides a powerful parallel for how meticulous planning and strategic spending can manage the inherent costs associated with significant transformations, fostering agility rather than enduring avoidable financial drains.

Spend to strengthen

It is crucial to differentiate between mere expenses and strategic investments. Some costs, when approached thoughtfully, represent direct investments that yield compounding returns. The evolution of Amazon Web Services (AWS) from an internal support function to a global, revenue-generating powerhouse illustrates how investing in core capabilities can create entirely new avenues of value. This principle emphasises the deliberate allocation of resources to build organisational robustness, cultivate key relationships and enhance foundational infrastructure, fostering anti-fragility and sustained competitive advantage rather than simply covering operational needs.

Build for visibility

Without comprehensive insight into spending patterns, strategic direction can become compromised. Spending that remains obscured or a culture that avoids open discussion about resource allocation can inadvertently steer an organisation toward unseen risks. Leveraging robust data analytics and intuitive dashboards can provide invaluable insights, yet the true power lies in distilling this information into actionable intelligence that sharpens strategic focus. Achieving this level of transparent understanding often requires dedicated effort to integrate disparate data sources and cultivate a culture of open inquiry.

Enough is a strategy

The pursuit of 'more' does not always equate to greater ambition; sometimes, it introduces unnecessary complexity and risk. Just as an individual might find greater financial freedom by defining 'enough' rather than pursuing maximal personal consumption, organisations can benefit profoundly from discerning what is optimal versus what is merely excessive. The disciplined approach of companies like 37Signals, choosing agility over unrestrained expansion, exemplifies how a clear understanding of 'enough' can lead to more focused efficiency, reduce unnecessary overhead and liberate resources for areas of genuine strategic impact. This principle encourages a deliberate pursuit of sufficiency over unbridled scale, leading to more resilient and purposeful growth.

In conclusion

Our smarter spending principles are not just about reducing cost, nor are they a checklist to complete. They are a lens though which you can increase clarity. They are mindful habits as much as they are operational tools. Together, they are not just a philosophy, but a playbook for purposeful, powerful change to help shape your everyday choices. The challenge now is not just to remember them, but to use them. You've seen what they can enable. Now it's up to you.

12.3 What stops us (and how to start anyway)

Organisational systems often favour momentum and expansion, sometimes resisting necessary adjustments. There are common internal dynamics that can impede the adoption of smarter spending practices. They are the very forces that might hold your organisation's potential in check, even when the principles for unlocking it are clear.

Understanding internal resistance

- *The hero leader:* A budget-holder strongly defends specific projects, sometimes driven by personal conviction, without sufficient scrutiny of broader organisational impact. This can arise from a lack of comprehensive *Visibility* into true return on investment, hindering the ability to *Spend with Purpose* strategically, or an implicit resistance to *Challenge Assumptions* about established initiatives.
- *Sandcastle syndrome*: This is the reluctance to dismantle or re-evaluate past investments, even when they no longer serve strategic goals. Organisations may cling to outdated systems or underperforming assets, protecting existing structures as conditions change. This dynamic can significantly impede the agility needed to *Control the Cost of Change* effectively and to *Challenge Assumptions* about prior commitments, often leading to prolonged inefficiencies.
- *The metrics mirage:* This describes a situation where performance is measured by easily quantifiable activities rather than genuine value or strategic outcome. Spending can appear justified on a dashboard but contribute minimally to core objectives. This represents a challenge in truly *Building for Visibility* of meaningful insights, diverting focus from assessing *Value before Cost* holistically.

Pathways to overcoming resistance

- *Culture audits:* Examine where and why questions about spending are encouraged or discouraged. Identifying areas where questioning is met with resistance can highlight underlying cultural barriers to *Challenge Assumptions* and foster greater *Build for Visibility*, crucial for deeper understanding.
- *Friction audits:* Analyse processes that make it easier to approve new spending than to question existing or historical expenditures. Streamlining the process for re-evaluation can promote more conscious *Spend with Purpose* and reveal hidden complexities in current operations.
- *Small wins playbook*: These small, tangible successes can build momentum for broader change, demonstrating the immediate benefits of a more intentional approach.

- *£10K in 10 days:* Identify and remove a dormant software license or an unused subscription. This quick win demonstrates the immediate benefits of applying *Enough is a Strategy* and improved *Build for Visibility* in practice.
- *'Oldest Contract First' review month*: Systematically re-evaluate long-standing vendor agreements. This forces a direct *Challenge Assumptions exercise* and a reassessment of current *Value before Cost*, often revealing significant uncaptured value.
- *'What would we not start today?' exercise:* If your organisation were to launch today, which existing projects or services would you intentionally choose not to initiate? This cuts through historical inertia and powerfully refocuses efforts on *Spend with Purpose*, highlighting areas that might no longer serve optimal strategic alignment.

Brief parables of missed opportunity

- *An innovation budget that remains consistently underspent:* An illustration of *Spend to Strengthen* being undermined by internal process hurdles, a lack of clear purpose in allocation, or an insufficient understanding of how to activate strategic investment.
- *A vendor rebate that goes unclaimed:* A challenge in *Building for Visibility* and *Seeing the Whole System*, representing lost value through oversight that might require specialised process optimisation to recover.
- *A significant contract renewed by default, without review:* A clear example of not *Challenging Assumptions* and a potential blind spot to *Value before Cost*, often due to the perceived effort involved in re-evaluation, hinting at deeper systemic inertia.

Culture undoubtedly influences spending habits, but gaining comprehensive visibility often reveals the most effective path to shifting that culture.

12.4 Get smart: Building a legacy of impact

Expanding our perspective, what does optimised business spending enable beyond your immediate enterprise? It supports greater resilience, fosters innovation and can contribute to a more effective allocation of resources across broader systems. When organisations manage their finances thoughtfully, applying principles like *See the Whole System* and *Sustainability is Survival*, it can create positive ripples that extend to communities and even national economies.

We sometimes observe striking contrasts that highlight the profound impact of spending choices.

- *A substantial executive away-day budget versus the resources needed to sustain a vital local service:* These comparisons are not for judgement, but to illustrate the potential impact of strategic resource allocation when viewed through a broader lens of *Spend with Purpose* and *Value before Cost*, considering the larger societal contribution and the cascading effects of how resources flow.
- *Corporate travel budgets that significantly exceed local educational funding needs:* Such examples underscore how refining spending priorities within organisations can free up capital for societal betterment, linking to the idea that *Profit Fuels Progress* when leveraged for wider positive impact, and that *Sustainability is Survival* can apply to social capital as well as environmental.

Consider macro examples for inspiration

- *Singapore:* Beyond its status as a financial centre, Singapore demonstrates a disciplined approach to long-term infrastructure investment, often with a multi-decade outlook. They exemplify *Spend with Purpose* and *Spend to Strengthen* on a national scale, recognising that present investment builds future competitive advantage and enduring national capability.
- *The Netherlands*: Their comprehensive flood management strategies serve as a powerful example of *Seeing the Whole System* and proactively *Controlling the Cost of Change* through strategic, preventative investments in integrated ecological and engineering solutions, rather than solely reacting to crises. This approach highlights how complex systemic challenges can be addressed through intentional spending.

Envisioning a future where smarter spending becomes a more pervasive practice

- *A smarter spend index*: Imagine a recognised framework to evaluate organisations' alignment with the ten smarter spending principles. This could foster greater transparency and incentivise purposeful, value-driven resource allocation across industries, signalling leadership in financial integrity.
- *SSP reporting integrated into ESG frameworks*: As Environmental, Social and Governance (ESG) reporting gains prominence, integrating smarter spending principles into these metrics could elevate financial integrity to the same level of importance as environmental stewardship and social responsibility. This

would allow *Sustainability is Survival* to be tracked and reported as a core business driver, demonstrating broader commitment.

Finally...

For organisations ready to move beyond initial insights to systemic, impactful transformation, deeper engagement can significantly accelerate results. While internal efforts are invaluable, addressing deeply entrenched issues or executing large-scale process redesign often benefits immensely from an objective, experienced perspective that can diagnose complex interdependencies, provide specialised methodologies and expedite comprehensive implementation.

Why not join the smarter spending network at www.smarterspending.co.uk. Connect with a community of leaders actively pursuing these principles.

You can explore bespoke workshops, toolkits, or diagnostic services and access specific category support, in the form of specialist expertise to tailor and accelerate your organisation's smarter spending journey.

Now you've smelled the smoke, the invitation is to share the burning sensation with everyone in your teams, because smarter spending starts when denial stops. This is not an endpoint; it is an invitation to a continuous pursuit of optimal value.

Embrace the depth of these principles. Their application promises not just enhanced efficiency, but a legacy of strategic integrity and profound impact. The era of smarter spending, and the future it builds, goes beyond business and begins with your commitment to see, to question, and to lead in a new direction.

Smarter spending is necessary, for businesses – and societies – to improve. Who will lead the charge? If you're reading this book, there's every chance it could be you. We certainly hope so.

Appendix

Activating smarter spending: Practical tools

This appendix is designed to help you transform the insights in this book into practical action. Our principles of smarter spending and the stories we've told help to provide a way of thinking. These tools aim to turn that mindset into a way of doing, enabling you, your team or the wider organisation to improve your approach to cost and supplier management.

These tools help to codify the knowledge that we've gained over the last 30 years. They are designed to spark reflection, facilitate discussion and guide action, whether for individual introspection, team reflections or broader company-wide strategic reviews. They are structured conversations and visual frameworks you can use to expose assumptions, challenge existing costs and processes and make smarter spending decisions.

They can be used by a company that turns over £5 million or £500 million, or by a single department trying to act more intelligently about how it allocates its resources. You will find four core tools here, each one supported by guidance and templates for action planning.

Use them all, or just the one you prefer. The only rule is to treat them as aids to spark debate, reveal insight and guide change.

A1 The smarter spending diagnostic and radar

Purpose:

Provide a quick visual snapshot of how well you adhere to smarter spending principles.

When to use it:

At the start of the process, to establish a baseline, then again at (quarterly, biannual) intervals to track progress. It can be completed individually but is best followed as a team discussion.

How to use it:

1. Review the ten principles and discuss.
2. Mark yourselves out of 10 for how much *control* and *clarity* you have and for how much there is a smarter spending *mindset*.
3. Plot the scores on a 10-point radar chart.
4. Connect the points to reveal your *smarter spending shape*.
5. Identify 2–3 areas with the lowest scores – these become your priority improvement areas.

Interpretation:

- A balanced radar with high scores indicates a healthy existing capability
- An uneven or spiky shape highlights blind spots, or areas to improve
- Repeating the exercise demonstrates improvement over time

Example:

A manufacturer scores itself low on *Build for Visibility* and *Control the Cost of Change*. Over the next 6 months, the firm budgets more accurately for the cost of change in their projects and shares data more openly between Finance and Operations. A later review demonstrates greater alignment between the two departments, which have led to increased understanding, more efficient processes and higher margins.

Radar diagram example:

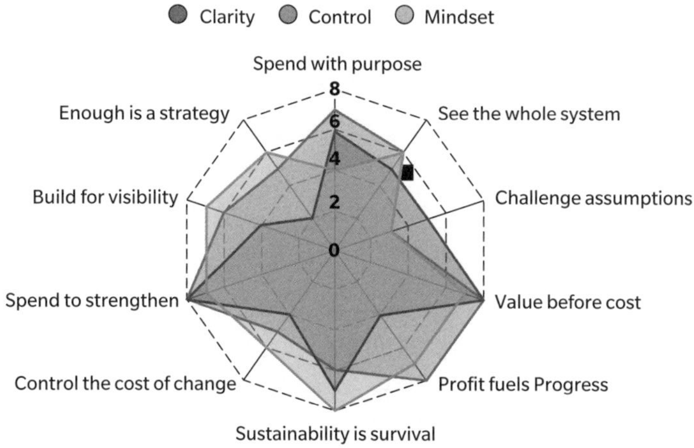

A2 The smarter spending matrix

Purpose:

To identify which spends or projects deliver the most value for the resources they consume, or where to focus, or how to compare control and visibility.

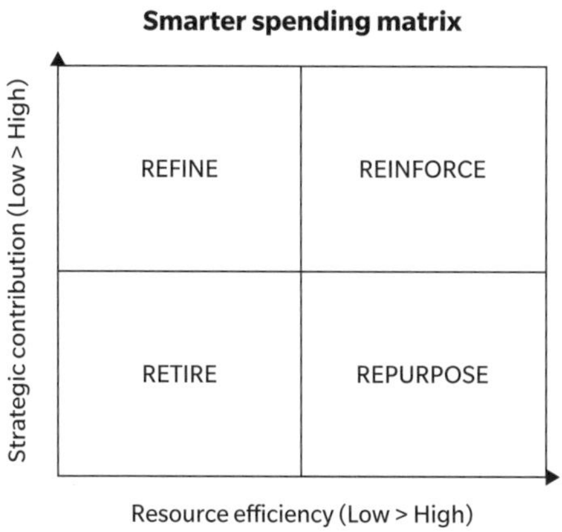

How to use it:

1. Choose 5–10 key spend areas or categories.
2. Manage a group discussion to place each on the grid.
3. Focus on the Refine and Repurpose zones first.
4. Record the actions for items in each quadrant.

Smaller businesses can use estimation and judgement during these discussions, but larger businesses should overlay this exercise with as much data as possible. *Cost to serve, ROI, strategic alignment scores etc.*

Definitions:

Zone	Description	Action	Example
Reinforce	Spending demonstrably supports core strategy and delivers results.	Protect and replicate. Share lessons with other areas of the business.	A fleet partner delivers high employee satisfaction scores, broad choices and sustainable financial and environmental savings.
Refine	Areas where inefficiency or complexity undermine value.	Simplify scope, streamline processes, or renegotiate contract design.	Regional marketing spend is split across multiple agencies. Strong impact, but poor coordination. Consolidating suppliers restores efficiency.
Repurpose	Well-managed spend that is not clearly strategic.	Redeploy the capability or resources elsewhere.	A print supplier provides fantastic service for low-value collateral. Pivots to provide branded tenders instead, resulting in more successful business development.
Retire	Spending that appears not to deliver meaningful impact.	Phase out, automate, or quit.	Multiple telecoms contracts inherited post-acquisition, all small and out of sync. Rationalising to a single supplier provides 20% saving and saves hours of staff admin.

Output:

A visual picture of where your resources are best deployed.

Recommendation:

Once you've mapped your categories on this matrix, you can go a step further and assess the practical *value potential* for savings in each area. This additional lens plots the amount of spending and potential savings at stake, against their accessibility: the ease of finding or delivering those savings.

Used together, the two perspectives give you both a strategic compass and a tactical map. The *smarter spending matrix* tells you what matters most. The *value potential* lens shows you where to start.

You can also use the matrix tool to plot other variables we've discussed in the book. Use it also to quantify Value vs Cost, the impact of Change vs Ease of implementation, Transparency vs Complexity and even purpose / value by using Systemic Impact vs Intentionality of Spend.

There are many other uses for this kind of tool. We are you sure you can find plenty of questions to ask yourselves in your organisation.

A3 The principle mapping canvas

Purpose:

To connect the ten principles of smarter spending to specific activities, decisions or behaviours in your business.

When to use it:

Planning phases, strategy reviews, post-project evaluations.

How to use it:

1 Draw a grid with ten boxes – name one for each principle.
2 For each box ask:
   (a) Where do we already live and breathe this principle?
   (b) Where do we fall shortest?
   (c) What evidence do have to prove it?
3 Score each principle out of 10 for maturity.
4 Highlight 2–3 principles for development.
5 Consider whether teams and departments can learn from others' activities or behaviours.

Output:

Participants will probably find the discussion itself the most valuable part of the exercise, uncovering as it will, previously unexplored areas for concern. Visually, the exercise will create a 'heat map' of cultural and operational strengths and weaknesses.

Spend with Purpose	8	Challenge Assumptions	6
See the Whole System	6	Value before Cost	7
Build for Visibility	4	Profit fuels Progress	8
Spend to Strengthen	6	Control the cost of Change	4
Sustainability is Survival	7	Enough is a Strategy	3

A4 The enough/optimal threshold exercise

Purpose:

To help leaders and teams to define what 'enough' is, to prevent over-engineering, complexity and waste. Uncovers where specifications, contract scopes or inherited decisions are no longer what is genuinely needed. Even good decisions at the time, left unexamined will accumulate drag. Many of these rafts will stay afloat longer than is necessary if you are not actively considering them. What is tying up employee time and costing you money?

When to use it:

During sourcing reviews, post-merger or acquisition, when trying to rationalise suppliers, or when prices are rising quicker than their value.

How to use it:

1 Select an area to review (e.g. Packaging, Insurance, Software licenses etc.).

2 Ask three questions:

   (a) Where might we be overpaying or overservicing without realising?

   (b) What level of performance, protection or specification is truly necessary?

   (c) What legacy decisions or inherited standards might be inflating costs?

3 Identify thresholds, where costs stop adding value.

4 Pilot lighter, or more tightly specified solutions in one area before attempting wider roll out.

Examples of 'enough' in practice:

Category	Hidden complexity	'Enough' Response	Result/Lesson
Packaging	Over-engineered secondary packaging used enterprise wide due to minimal fragile product lines.	Introduce packaging specification by utility, using lighter, recyclable board for most SKUs.	15% saving, reduced storage requirements.
Energy & Utilities	Inherited office energy contracts had been auto renewed on non-competitive terms.	Consolidate contracts, align renewal dates, retender with combined volumes leverage.	12% saving, simplified reporting and accounting procedures due to single supplier relationship.
Professional Services	Legacy consulting retainers kept on 'just in case'.	Replace with ad hoc support as necessary.	Six-figure annual savings, with capability retained.
Real-world example			
The Body Shop – Anita Roddick	Shunned the heavy luxury cosmetics packaging she encountered in the industry.	Switched to refillable recyclable bottles, minimal packaging and local sourcing.	Reduced material costs and created a new environmental standard for retail.
Dame Ellen MacArthur Foundation	Realised the linear economy 'take, make and dispose' model wases capital and resources.	Embraced the circular economy to ensure materials circulate at their enough threshold and are reused, repaired and regenerated.	Global impact on manufacturing and policy. Countless firms adopting circular principles that cut raw materials dependency and cost.

Output:

A threshold statement / boundary specification model for each category. For example, 'Packaging must adhere to X, Y, Z as a minimum standard. Additional reinforcement requires justification and approval.'

Gather these together to create a smarter spending threshold register.

Reflection questions for each principle

Designed to initiate thoughtful dialogue around each principle. Honest self-assessment and open discussion is encouraged. Only by uncovering these challenges can the first steps to effective solutions be taken.

1 Spend with purpose:

- *Business:* 'For your top three expenditures last quarter, how explicitly were they aligned with your company's strategic goals or values? Could that alignment be made more transparent or stronger?'
- *Team discussion:* 'How effectively do we currently communicate the "purpose" behind significant team or departmental spending? Is this purpose clearly understood and agreed upon by everyone involved, or is there ambiguity that could lead to misallocation?'

2 See the whole system:

- *Business:* 'Identify one process where spending occurs across multiple departments (e.g., software licensing, external legal services). How much visibility do you currently have into the total cost and holistic impact across the entire operational flow? What unseen costs might exist between the cracks?'
- *Team discussion:* 'Where do our current data or operational silos prevent us from gaining a complete financial picture of a key project or operational area? What complexities emerge when we try to connect the dots?'

3 Challenge assumptions:

- *Business:* 'What's one long-standing spending practice in your organisation that has rarely been questioned? What fundamental premise supports its continuation, and what might happen if that premise no longer holds true?'
- *Team discussion:* 'What embedded practices in our purchasing or resource allocation do we accept without deep interrogation? How might an objective newcomer or a seasoned external expert view them differently?'

4 Value before cost:

- *Business:* 'For your last major vendor contract, beyond the direct price, what were the three most critical "value" elements you sought (e.g., long-term reliability, innovation potential, comprehensive support, strategic partnership)? How are you measuring the tangible impact of these non-cost benefits?'
- *Team discussion:* 'How can we shift our team's procurement conversations from solely focusing on "cost" to robust "value" discussions with both internal stakeholders and external partners? What metrics are we missing?'

5 Profit fuels progress:

- *Business:* 'How clearly do your teams understand that strategic investment (spending) is essential for future profitability and sustained growth, rather than viewing profit as a separate, distant goal?'
- *Team discussion:* 'In what ways might our current budgeting processes inadvertently deter strategic spending that, though incurring an initial outlay, could lead to greater long-term value creation or profit generation?'

6 Sustainability is survival:

- *Business:* 'Identify one area where investing in more sustainable practices (e.g., energy efficiency, resource circularity, reduced waste streams) could yield measurable financial savings and enhanced brand reputation in the next 1–3 years. What barriers currently prevent this investment?'
- *Team discussion:* 'Beyond compliance, how can we proactively integrate broader sustainability goals into our spending decisions to create both environmental benefits and long-term financial value for the organisation?'

7 Control the cost of change:

- *Business:* 'Reflect on a recent significant organisational change. What unforeseen "costs" (financial, operational, human) emerged that were not fully anticipated? How might more proactive, strategic spending have mitigated these, or even turned them into opportunities?'
- *Team discussion:* 'How can we build a "change budget" or contingency into our project planning that focuses on smoothing transitions and maximising adoption, rather than simply reacting to unexpected failures or resistance?'

8 Spend to strengthen:

- *Business:* 'Where are you making "transactional" purchases when a "strategic investment" in a new capability, talent development, or a deeper relationship could deliver significantly greater, compounding returns for the organisation?'

- *Team discussion:* 'Are we adequately investing in the tools, training, or partnerships that genuinely strengthen our team's core competencies and build long-term organisational resilience, or are we consistently choosing short-term fixes?'

9 Build for visibility:

- *Business:* 'If you needed to know the total spend on a specific category (e.g., professional services, cloud infrastructure, specific raw materials) yesterday, how quickly and accurately could you consolidate that comprehensive data?'
- *Team discussion:* 'What are the top three data points related to spending that, if made instantly visible and understandable to our team, would most improve our strategic decision-making and accountability?'

10 Enough is a strategy:

- *Business:* 'Where is your organisation potentially over-investing in "maximal" or overly complex solutions when a more "optimal" solution would suffice and free up valuable resources for other strategic priorities?'
- *Team discussion:* 'In what areas do we implicitly equate "more" with "better", when a clear definition of "enough" – or even "less" – could lead to greater efficiency, reduced complexity and ultimately, a more focused impact?'

Creating an action plan

At the end of any sessions when using these tools, take 10 minutes to agree what comes next.

Principle/ Issue	Action	Owner	Timeline	Expected outcome
Build for Visibility	Consolidate supplier spending data into a shared Power BI Dashboard	IT Director	Q3 2026	Greater transparency for earlier issue flagging and more efficient decision-making.

Example

Keep it simple – 3 or 4 actions are enough.
Review quarterly or biannually using the diagnostics radar.

Closing note

Use these tools, but feel free to adapt them to suit your purposes. Whatever the outputs are, they are not rules you must never break. You can choose to live by them, but you can also choose to ignore them when they don't make sense for you. Use them to lift your enterprise up, not to knock it down.

Ther power of these tools lies in the conversations they generate, the clarity those conversations create and the ideas they stimulate. Smarter spending is not designed to be a financial process – it's a way of seeing. We hope that using these tools provides you with a new lens, through which you can see your expenditure with sharper focus. You might want to see how they apply to your household expenses or even consider what adopting them might do for society.

Index